THE
ICE CREAM
&
FROZEN YOGURT

COOKBOOK

THE ICE CREAM & FROZEN YOGURT

COOKBOOK

Enjoy Homemade Ice Creams,
Frozen Yogurts, Sorbets,
Sherbets, and More

by Mable and Gar Hoffman

RUNNING PRESS
PHILADELPHIA · LONDON

© 2004 by Running Press
All rights reserved under the Pan-American and International Copyright Conventions
Printed in the United States

This book may not be reproduced in whole or in part, in any form or by any means, electronic or
mechanical, including photocopying, recording, or by any information storage and retrieval system now
known or hereafter invented, without written permission from the publisher.

9   8   7   6   5   4   3   2   1
Digit on the right indicates the number of this printing

Library of Congress Control Number: 2003095208

ISBN 0-7624-1829-X
Cover design by Toby Schmidt
Cover photography © Brand X Photography
Interior design by Bob Anderson
Typography: TheSans and TheSerif

Originally published as *Ice Cream & Frozen Yogurt*
© 2000 Fisher Books

This book may be ordered by mail from the publisher. Please include $2.50 for postage and handling.
But try your bookstore first!

Running Press Book Publishers
125 South Twenty-second Street
Philadelphia, Pennsylvania 19103-4399

Visit us on the web!
www.runningpress.com

Contents

Ice Cream, Frozen Yogurt, & Frozen Desserts

EVERYBODY LOVES ICE CREAM. Many of us have fond childhood memories of visiting ice cream parlors or soda fountains, most of which have been replaced in recent years by ice cream and frozen-yogurt take-out shops. These emporiums boast all sorts of flavor combinations. With so many wonderful choices, it can be difficult to settle on only one or two flavors at a time. You may experience some of that same indecision when you first decide which of these recipes to try. Be diligent and try many; we think you will find many new favorites.

Even though ice cream remains our nation's favorite dessert, we have seen the popularity of frozen yogurt grow since it was first introduced in the 1970s. Perhaps the interest in frozen yogurt is the result of people being more concerned about eating healthfully, because frozen yogurt is available in low-fat varieties. Whatever the reason, it's almost as easy to find frozen-yogurt shops these days as it is to find ice cream shops. Both offer customers immediate satisfaction and some extremely creative taste sensations.

With so many frozen products so readily available commercially, you might question the impulse to make your own. There are many advantages to making your own frozen desserts. You can make a wide variety of ice creams at about half the cost of those commercially produced. You do not have to leave home to get it. Ice cream making is pretty easy. Friends and family can join in and help—it's fun!

Another benefit to making your own ice cream or frozen yogurt is that you select the ingredients. You can eliminate or control most chemical emulsifiers, stabilizers, and artificial flavors that are found in most commercial products. Because many people cannot enjoy ice cream or frozen yogurt because of food allergies, we have created recipes that will fit within their diets, such as egg-free and dairy-free frozen dishes. For those of us who do not follow restricted diets, we have emphasized using fresh fruits in combination with different dairy products. Whether you desire rich cream, an icy sorbet, or a lighter, low-fat yogurt, you'll find a luscious recipe for it within these pages.

Many cooks wonder if they can substitute yogurt for cream in a recipe to make frozen yogurt instead of ice cream. Yogurt and cream have different properties. As a rule, ice cream is made from a cooked custard base, which is cooled and frozen. Yogurt, however, is not cooked before using, because it is susceptible to curdling when heated. Generally, we combine all yogurt ingredients cold and then freeze them. Also, yogurt must be combined with other dairy products or juices to insure a smooth, light result. Used alone, it becomes hard and cannot be spooned easily.

Not Just for Dessert

Our eating styles change from time to time, and we can take advantage of that to serve frozen dishes a little differently. Not all of the recipes in this book are meant for dessert. When entertaining, consider serving Gazpacho Frappé as the first course or a refreshing Grapefruit-Mint Granita between courses. A small scoop presented in an attractive glass dish or tiny goblet makes a big impression on guests.

Dessert choices are almost limitless—anything from a plain scoop of ice cream, unadorned, to the lavish garnishing of a Banana Split. And for warm summer days, can anything be more inviting on a hot afternoon than a cool taste of creamy Piña Colada? We don't need a special or event to satisfy our desire for a frozen treat. Any day can be an ice cream day!

So Many Choices

This book is divided into chapters by flavor to save you time in searching for and comparing recipes. For instance, if you love chocolate, choose from rich Fudge Ice Cream, Chocolate Sherbet, Rocky Road Ice Cream, Chocolate Frozen Yogurt, or Toasted Almond Fudge Frozen Yogurt. Our aim is to offer you delicious options featuring your favorite flavors and to introduce you to new combinations.

Citrus fruits are especially versatile in desserts; not only are they delicious alone, but they lend distinct flavor to other fruit combinations. Scooped-out orange, lemon, or grapefruit halves make excellent serving bowls for the final product. Fill them hours or a day ahead, and you will be prepared to present your guests with a visual as well as a taste treat. Garnish just before serving with a dollop of whipped cream, a sprig of fresh mint, or a candied violet.

Fresh berries are another boon. We are no longer confined to seasonal availability, but can make berry ice cream year-round. Fresh berries provide frozen desserts with an incredible range of color as well as flavor. You may choose to remove the larger seeds from berries such as blackberry, raspberry, or boysenberry. Most people do not find strawberry seeds objectionable.

Tropical and exotic fruits, such as papaya, guava, and mangoes, pair nicely with more traditional flavors.

Can you imagine a birthday party without ice cream? Chapter 9 provides recipes and tips for making special treats for children of all ages. Entertaining is easier when you prepare one of our frozen pies, cakes, or molded creations in advance. Prepare them in attractive serving pans or individual molds, cover with heavy plastic wrap or foil and freeze until needed. For another memorable finale, surprise your dinner guests with Acapulco Mocha Pie or Apricot-Ginger Cheesecake.

> Feel free to add cookies, candies, and nuts to your frozen dessert. They lend unexpected texture as well as flavor.

Not to be forgotten are everybody's favorite: soda fountain specialties. We help you create your own soda fountain favorites at home. With only a little practice, you can amaze your friends and family with irresistible frozen creations. Recipes for toppings, sauces, after-dinner drinks, and more are all here, simple to make and wonderful to present and eat. So go ahead—enjoy ice cream and frozen yogurt whenever the mood strikes!

THE SCOOP ON FROZEN DESSERTS

Bombe. The name comes from a ridged, melon-shaped mold called a bombe that is about the size of a cantaloupe. Bombes are usually layered with two or more flavors of ice cream, sherbet or frozen yogurt.

Frappé. Similar to ices, frappés are not frozen solid but served while still slushy.

Frozen mousse. Rich in eggs and cream, this smooth mixture requires no stirring as it freezes. Beaten egg whites or whipped cream are folded into the custard-like base. The mixture is usually frozen in a bowl or mold.

Frozen soufflé. Similar to a mousse, this light, creamy mixture is frozen and served in a soufflé dish.

Frozen yogurt. Made from plain, flavored, low-fat, or fat-free yogurt, combined with fruit, sweeteners, milk and flavorings.

Gelato. The Italian word for ice cream. Gelato contains less air than American ice cream, and has a denser texture.

Ice cream. A frozen mixture with a high butterfat content, rich with cream, milk, sweeteners and flavorings.

Ice or granita. These are the relatives of French sorbets. They are made of puréed fruits or fruit juices and a sweetener. They must be stirred while freezing, or the frozen mixture must be scraped with a fork or beaten in a food processor.

Parfait. Layers of ice cream, sauce, whipped cream, and fruits or nuts, served in tall, clear glasses.

Sherbets. Generally sherbets have a lower fat content, which affects the texture, making it icy rather than smooth as in ice cream. Milk instead of cream is used in sherbets. They also contain fruits or fruit juices and sugar or another sweetener. Unflavored gelatin may be added to give a lighter texture.

Sorbets. French sorbets are similar to American-style ices. They never contain milk or eggs. Sorbets are frozen combinations of puréed fruits, fruit juices, and sweeteners. They must be stirred or agitated during freezing to reduce ice crystals. These ices become light and fluffy when beaten in a food processor with the metal blade. Sorbets are best eaten immediately after freezing.

INGREDIENTS

Dairy Products

Buttermilk is thicker and lower in calories than whole milk. Its slightly tangy flavor is excellent in some ice creams, such as peach.

Dairy sour cream is found in the dairy section of supermarkets. Its slightly tart flavor and smooth, thick texture make it an ideal ice cream ingredient.

Evaporated milk is more concentrated than whole fresh milk, giving a richer taste and smoother texture to ice cream. We use it undiluted.

Fat-free milk, also called nonfat or skim milk, contains little or no fat. It is used in low-fat recipes.

Half-and-half is a mixture of milk and cream and is often called light cream. It provides limited richness to ice cream but is not heavy enough to be whipped.

Milk is the basic ingredient of ice cream. When a recipe calls for milk, use fresh whole homogenized milk.

Nonfat dry milk powder is economical and needs no refrigeration until it is reconstituted.

Sweetened condensed milk should not be confused with evaporated milk. This is concentrated milk with a large amount of sugar added for flavor. Used undiluted, it provides a smooth texture and gives ice cream a unique flavor.

Whipping cream is heavy. When whipped, the cream traps air in tiny pockets, which increases its volume. Unwhipped or whipped, it produces a smooth, very rich ice cream.

Yogurt is milk that has fermented and coagulated by the addition of certain strains of beneficial bacteria. You may use plain, flavored, low-fat, or nonfat yogurt in the recipes in this book.

Thickening and Flavoring Ingredients

Cornstarch is used in the cooked mixtures as a thickening agent sometimes and to help make a smooth product. Cook these mixtures the recommended length of time to eliminate the flavor of uncooked starch.

Eggs are an important ingredient in ice cream. They thicken custard-type mixtures and provide a light texture when beaten. We used large eggs. In recipes directing you to beat eggs slightly, use a fork or whisk and beat until blended into one color.

Extracts and flavorings. When making any frozen dessert, use pure extracts whenever possible rather than artificial flavoring.

Honey provides a distinctive flavor. It may have a slight orange, clover, or sage flavor.

Light corn syrup is used with sugar in the fruit ices, sherbets, and sorbets. It gives a light, smooth texture.

Maple syrup in these recipes refers to maple-flavored pancake syrup. Genuine maple syrup will give your ice cream a richer flavor.

Marshmallows and marshmallow creme each have a gelatin base and a light texture. Including either will give your ice cream a smoother texture.

Unflavored gelatin helps create a smoother texture. A word of caution: Each envelope contains about one tablespoon unflavored gelatin. Some recipes require only one teaspoon to make a very good product. Do not use more than the recipe calls for!

ICE CREAM MAKERS

Ice cream machines, which are also used to make frozen yogurt and ices, have improved dramatically since the days of the hand-cranked, wooden-tub models. Now they're lighter and more efficient. Many are powered by electric motors. The price of ice cream makers varies according to their size and complexity. The newer self-refrigerant machines truly make it effortless to create your own dessert. If you use a reliable recipe and follow the manufacturer's operating instructions, all machines will produce a very good quality ice cream or frozen yogurt.

Perhaps the most popular traditional style ice cream maker uses a combination of ice and salt (called brine) as a freezing agent or refrigerant. A good ratio of salt to ice is 2 cups salt to 8 pounds of ice cubes or crushed ice. Machines are available in many sizes; the most popular range from 1 quart to 2 gallons. The size indicates the amount of ice cream it can make at a time. These machines are available in both hand-cranked and motor-driven models.

The second type of ice cream maker features an ice cream canister with liquid refrigerant sealed between the double walls of the canister. The canister must be placed in a refrigerator-freezer for 8 to 10 hours to freeze the liquid refrigerant. Ingredients are poured into the canister. A dasher in the canister is cranked by hand or by using an electric motor. These machines are available in two sizes: 1 pint and 1 quart.

The third type of ice cream maker is the most convenient to use by far. This type contains a sealed fluorocarbon refrigerant system and electromechanical mechanisms similar to those in home refrigerators and freezers. To use these machines, pour the ingredients into the canister and turn on the machine—the freezing process is underway! These machines make about 1 to 1½ quarts in approximately 30 minutes.

> **BRINE RECIPE**
>
> Use a combination of salt and ice. A good ratio of salt to ice is 2 cups salt to 8 pounds of ice cubes or crushed ice.

REFRIGERATOR-FREEZER STILL FREEZING

If you don't have an ice cream maker, you can make ice cream in the freezer compartment of your refrigerator. This method is called *still freezing*. Because this method does not continuously agitate the ice cream during the freezing process, the quantity and texture varies slightly from that produced in an ice cream maker. For a smoother and creamier product by this method, beat the mixture two or three times during the freezing process.

1. Food-Processor Technique

Pour prepared ingredients into a loaf pan or 8-inch-square baking pan, cover with foil or plastic wrap, and place in freezer. Freeze until solid (1 to 2 hours). Break frozen mixture into pieces; spoon into a food processor fitted with a metal blade. Process until soft but not melted. Repeat freezing and processing one or two more times, if desired.

2. Mixer Technique

Pour prepared ice cream ingredients into a metal mixer bowl, cover with foil or plastic wrap, and place in freezer. Freeze about 2 hours or until ice cream is firm at the edges and semisoft in the center. Beat with electric mixer on medium-high speed until soft but not melted. Repeat freezing and beating one or two more times, if desired.

After final processing or beating, stir or fold in any whole or chopped nuts, pieces of candy or cookies and pieces of fruit or prepared ingredients you choose to produce a swirled or marbled effect. Serve after final beating, or return to freezer and serve later.

QUANTITIES

For each recipe we give an estimated amount the recipe makes, such as "Makes about 1 quart." We say "about" because many factors affect the ultimate yield of the recipe. The ingredients, the freezing method and the temperature of the prepared ingredients prior to freezing all relate to the final quantity. Ingredients such as cream, half-and-half, eggs, and gelatin tend to increase the yield. Also the volume of the frozen mixture exceeds the volume of the prepared ingredients in their liquid state prior to freezing. (This is known as overrun in the ice cream industry.)

When the mixture is frozen in an ice cream maker with a dasher, air is whipped into it. This too increases the volume (and also enhances the smoothness of the ice cream). If the temperature of the prepared ingredients is below 40F (5C) when the freezing begins, the mixture will freeze too quickly, and a minimal amount of air will be incorporated; thus, the volume will not increase significantly and the ice cream will probably contain large ice crystals.

Many people prefer to ripen (harden) the ice cream before serving. Ripening firms the mixture and give flavors time to blend. Always ripen molded frozen desserts. If you have prepared your recipe using an ice cream maker, follow the manufacturer's directions for firming ice cream.

To ripen ice cream in brine, drain off excess water and then replace what was melted and removed with more ice and salt. Cover canister and bucket with a blanket or newspaper. Let ripen 1 to 3 hours.

STORING AND SOFTENING FROZEN DESSERTS

To store your frozen creation, spoon the mixture into an airtight container. This is especially important if the freezer is a frost-free type. The same process that removes moisture from the freezer compartment also removes moisture from improperly protected foods. Plastic containers are excellent for storing.

Cover molded ice cream, pies, and cakes with foil or plastic wrap while they are ripening in the freezer. If the product will be in the freezer longer than 8 to 10 hours, wrap the entire container in foil, making an airtight package. Or place the product in a freezer bag and seal. This prevents the formation of large ice crystals. Place ice cream sandwiches and bonbons in rigid containers, or wrap tightly in foil or seal in freezer bags.

Because homemade ice creams contain few or none of the stabilizers in commercial products, they will become significantly harder than their commercial counterparts when stored in a refrigerator freezer. Check the firmness of the frozen product about 1 hour before serving time.

Serving Portions

One quart will serve 6 to 8 adults. Plan 8 to 10 servings per quart when serving à la mode. However, for teens, 4 to 5 servings per quart is more realistic.

How Recipes Were Tested

Food values for all commercially packaged ingredients used in these recipes, such as candies, are listed as they appear on product labels. In a few cases, we indicated brand names so you would know the exact product we used.

Nutritional information is based on ingredients listed as a first choice, if options were provided (such as using liqueur or

---

STORAGE TIPS

Do not store ice cream in a glass container.

Ice cream is best when stored at about 15F (10C). It will be firm but pliable enough to dip and serve.

Press a piece of plastic film against the exposed ice cream surface before the lid is attached. This provides a good seal against moisture being removed and minimizes ice-crystal formation. Without this extra seal, the surface of the ice cream will dry out.

The best way to soften ice cream is to place it in the refrigerator 15 to 20 minutes before serving time.

The quickest way to soften hard ice cream is to process it in a food processor until fluffy but not thawed.

You can also spoon the hard ice cream into a chilled mixer bowl and beat on medium-high speed until fluffy but not thawed.

fruit juice). Optional choices are not included. Serving portions are 8 per quart, or the higher number is used for the range in servings.

Documentation

Nutrient analysis was calculated using The Food Processor II Nutrition & Diet Analysis System software program, by ESHA Research. Additionally, nutritional data provided by food manufacturers was used for some specialty items, such as candies.

Legend:

Cal = Calories
Carb = Carbohydrates calculated in grams
Fat calculated in grams
Chol = Cholesterol calculated in milligrams
Calcium calculated in milligrams

Vanilla

ICE CREAM

Old-Fashioned Vanilla Ice Cream
French-Vanilla Ice Cream
Fat-Free Vanilla Ice Cream
Coconut-Vanilla-Pudding Ice Cream
Royal Vanilla Ice Cream
Soft Vanilla Ice Cream

FROZEN YOGURT

Basic Vanilla Frozen Yogurt
Traditional Vanilla Frozen Yogurt
Vanilla Supreme Frozen Yogurt
Healthful Vanilla Frozen Yogurt
Crème Brûlée Frozen Yogurt

Old-Fashioned Vanilla Ice Cream

SMOOTH AND CREAMY! OF ALL THE RECIPES IN THIS CHAPTER, THE HOFFMAN FAMILY VOTED THIS AS THEIR ALL-TIME FAVORITE.

Makes about 2 quarts

- 1⅓ cups sugar
- 1 tablespoon cornstarch
- ¼ teaspoon salt
- 3 cups milk
- 2 egg yolks
- 1 (5-ounce) can evaporated milk
- 1 cup whipping cream
- 1 tablespoon vanilla extract

IN A MEDIUM SAUCEPAN, combine sugar, cornstarch, and salt. Stir in milk. Stir over medium heat. Simmer 1 minute over low heat; set aside. In a small bowl, lightly beat egg yolks. Stir about 1 cup milk mixture into egg yolks. Stirring constantly, pour egg-yolk mixture into remaining milk mixture. Cook and stir over low heat 2 minutes or until slightly thickened. Add evaporated milk, whipping cream, and vanilla. Cool to room temperature. Pour into ice cream canister. Freeze in ice cream maker according to manufacturer's directions; or follow refrigerator-freezer instructions on page 11.

1 serving contains:

Cal	Carb	Fat	Chol	Calcium
216	28g	10g	71mg	124mg

French-Vanilla Ice Cream

**CHOOSE THIS CLASSIC WHEN YOU WANT TO CONCLUDE A FINE DINNER
WITH AN OUTSTANDING, YET SIMPLE, DESSERT.**

Makes about 2 quarts

- 3 cups half-and-half
- 1 cup sugar
- 4 egg yolks, beaten
- 1 cup whipping cream
- 1 tablespoon vanilla extract

IN A HEAVY MEDIUM SAUCEPAN, combine half-and-half, sugar, and beaten egg yolks. Cook and stir over low heat until mixture coats a spoon and is slightly thickened. Cool to room temperature. Stir in whipping cream and vanilla. Pour into ice cream canister. Freeze in ice cream maker according to manufacturer's directions; or follow refrigerator-freezer instructions on page 11.

1 serving contains:

Cal	Carb	Fat	Chol	Calcium
234	20g	16g	120mg	84mg

Fat-Free Vanilla Ice Cream

ENJOY A GUILT-FREE TREAT! THIS ICE CREAM IS LESS RICH BUT STILL VERY SATISFYING.

Makes about 2 quarts

- ½ cup sugar
- 2 tablespoons cornstarch
- ⅛ teaspoon salt
- 5 cups fat-free or low-fat milk
- ½ cup light corn syrup
- 2 eggs
- 1 tablespoon vanilla extract

IN A MEDIUM SAUCEPAN, combine sugar, cornstarch, and salt. Gradually stir in milk and corn syrup. Cook and stir over low heat until mixture is slightly thickened; set aside. In a small bowl, beat eggs. Stir about 1 cup hot-milk mixture into beaten eggs. Stirring constantly, pour egg mixture into remaining milk mixture. Stir over low heat until bubbly, 4 to 5 minutes. Cool to room temperature; stir in vanilla. Pour into ice cream canister. Freeze in ice cream maker according to manufacturer's directions; or follow refrigerator-freezer instructions on page 11.

1 serving contains:

Cal	Carb	Fat	Chol	Calcium
126	25g	1g	37mg	130mg

Coconut-Vanilla-Pudding Ice Cream

COCONUT ADDS TEXTURE TO THE OTHERWISE SMOOTH CONSISTENCY OF THIS EASY-TO-MAKE TREAT.

Makes about 1 quart

- ¼ cup sugar
- 1 (3½-ounce) package instant vanilla pudding mix
- ½ cup low-fat milk
- 1 cup half-and-half
- ¼ cup flaked coconut

IN A MEDIUM BOWL, combine ingredients. Whisk briefly to blend. Pour into ice cream canister. Freeze in ice cream maker according to manufacturer's directions; or follow refrigerator-freezer instructions on page 11.

1 serving contains:

Cal	Carb	Fat	Chol	Calcium
178	27g	7g	17mg	68mg

Royal Vanilla Ice Cream

A TRULY REGAL VANILLA ICE CREAM, WHICH IS WONDERFUL SERVED PLAIN OR TOPPED WITH THE FRESHEST SEASONAL FRUIT.

Makes about 1 quart

5	egg yolks
⅔	cup sugar
1	cup half-and-half
2	tablespoons butter
1	cup whipping cream
2	teaspoons vanilla extract

IN A MEDIUM BOWL, beat egg yolks and sugar until well blended. Pour into top of a double boiler. Stir in half-and-half. Cook and stir over gently boiling water until mixture thickens. Remove from heat. Stir in butter. Stirring occasionally, cool on a rack about 15 minutes. Stir in whipping cream and vanilla. Pour into ice cream canister. Freeze in ice cream maker according to manufacturer's directions; or follow refrigerator-freezer instructions on page 11.

1 serving contains:

Cal	Carb	Fat	Chol	Calcium
362	25g	27g	257mg	88mg

Soft Vanilla Ice Cream

NOW YOU CAN CREATE A SOFT, SMOOTH TEXTURE SIMILAR TO THAT OF COMMERCIAL SOFT ICE CREAM.

Makes about 1 quart

½	teaspoon unflavored gelatin
1	tablespoon water
1	cup low-fat milk
½	cup instant nonfat dry milk
½	cup sugar
1½	cups half-and-half or whipping cream
½	teaspoon vanilla extract

IN A MEDIUM SAUCEPAN, sprinkle gelatin over cold water; let stand one minute. Stir over very low heat until gelatin dissolves. Gradually add low-fat milk. Stir in dry milk and sugar; then half-and-half or whipping cream and vanilla. Pour into ice cream canister. Freeze in ice cream maker according to manufacturer's directions; or follow refrigerator-freezer instructions on page 11. Serve when mixture is firm enough to hold soft peaks.

1 serving contains:

Cal	Carb	Fat	Chol	Calcium
189	24g	7g	34mg	181mg

Basic Vanilla Frozen Yogurt

SO SMOOTH, YOU'LL NEVER GUESS IT'S MADE WITH YOGURT.

Makes about 1 quart

- ⅔ cup sugar
- 2 teaspoons cornstarch
- 1 (12-ounce) can evaporated low-fat milk
- 1 egg, slightly beaten
- 2 tablespoons light corn syrup
- 2 teaspoons vanilla extract
- 1½ cups plain low-fat yogurt, stirred

IN A MEDIUM SAUCEPAN, combine sugar and cornstarch. Stir in milk, beaten egg, and corn syrup. Cook and stir over low heat until mixture is thickened and coats a metal spoon. Remove from heat; cool. Stir in vanilla and yogurt. Freeze in ice cream maker according to manufacturer's directions; or follow refrigerator-freezer instructions on page 11.

1 serving contains:

Cal	Carb	Fat	Chol	Calcium
217	39g	3g	50mg	280mg

Traditional Vanilla Frozen Yogurt

USE THIS AS THE BASE FOR EXOTIC FROZEN DRINKS, FAVORITE SUNDAES AND OTHER SODA-FOUNTAIN TREATS.

| Makes about 1 quart |

- 1½   cups low-fat milk
- 1   teaspoon unflavored gelatin
- ½   cup sugar
- 3   tablespoons light corn syrup
- 1½   teaspoons vanilla extract
- 1½   cups plain low-fat yogurt

IN A SMALL SAUCEPAN, combine milk and gelatin; let stand 1 minute. Stir over low heat until gelatin dissolves. Combine with sugar, corn syrup, and vanilla. Stir in yogurt. Freeze in ice cream maker according to manufacturer's directions; or follow refrigerator-freezer instructions on page 11.

1 serving contains:

Cal	Carb	Fat	Chol	Calcium
168	32g	2g	9mg	180mg

Vanilla Supreme Frozen Yogurt

A CREAMY-LIGHT TEXTURE COMES FROM THE ADDITION OF BEATEN EGG WHITE.

Makes about 1 quart

½	cup low-fat milk
1	teaspoon unflavored gelatin
¾	cup sugar
1½	teaspoons vanilla extract
1½	cups plain low-fat yogurt, stirred
1	egg white
⅓	cup water
⅓	cup nonfat dry milk

IN A SMALL SAUCEPAN, combine low-fat milk and gelatin; let stand 1 minute. Cook and stir over low heat until gelatin dissolves; cool. In medium bowl, combine sugar, vanilla, and yogurt; stir in dissolved gelatin mixture. In another medium bowl, combine egg white, water, and nonfat dry milk. Beat until stiff but not dry. Fold into yogurt mixture. Freeze in ice cream maker according to manufacturer's directions; or follow refrigerator-freezer instructions on page 11.

1 serving contains:

Cal	Carb	Fat	Chol	Calcium
166	32g	1g	6mg	186mg

Healthful Vanilla Frozen Yogurt

FOR THOSE WATCHING THEIR DIETS, WE OFFER THIS BASIC RECIPE.

Makes about 1 quart

1½	cups fat-free or low-fat milk
⅔	cup sugar
2	tablespoons light corn syrup
1	(8-ounce) carton egg substitute (Egg Beaters®), thawed
1½	teaspoons vanilla extract
1	cup plain fat-free or low-fat yogurt, stirred

IN A 2-QUART SAUCEPAN, combine milk, sugar, and corn syrup. Add egg substitute; stir until well blended. Cook and stir over moderate heat until mixture is very thick. Remove from heat; cool. Add vanilla and yogurt. Freeze in ice cream maker according to manufacturer's directions; or follow refrigerator-freezer instructions on page 11.

1 serving made with fat-free milk and fat-free yogurt contains:

Cal	Carb	Fat	Chol	Calcium
177	34g	1g	2mg	146mg

1 serving made with low-fat milk and low-fat yogurt contains:

Cal	Carb	Fat	Chol	Calcium
198	34g	3g	8mg	163mg

Crème Brûlée Frozen Yogurt

A VERSATILE RECIPE TO ENJOY IN A VARIETY OF WAYS. FOR HOLIDAY ENTERTAINING, THIS MAKES EXCELLENT EGGNOG FROZEN YOGURT. SIMPLY SUBSTITUTE A LIGHT DUSTING OF GROUND NUTMEG FOR THE BRÛLÉE TOPPING.

Makes about 1 quart

BRÛLÉE TOPPING:

- ⅓ cup lightly packed brown sugar
- 1 tablespoon orange liqueur
- 1 or 2 dashes ground cloves

FROZEN YOGURT:

- 1¼ cups fat-free milk
- 3 beaten eggs or 6 ounces egg substitute (Egg Beaters®), thawed
- ¾ cup granulated sugar
- ⅛ teaspoon ground cinnamon
- ¼ teaspoon salt, optional
- 2 teaspoons vanilla extract
- 1¼ cups plain fat-free yogurt, stirred

Brûlée Topping: In small bowl, break up any brown sugar lumps with a fork or spoon. Add liqueur and cloves; mix thoroughly. Refrigerate in covered container until consumed.

Frozen Yogurt: In 1½-quart heavy saucepan, combine milk, eggs, granulated sugar, cinnamon, and salt, if desired. Cook and stir over low heat 10 minutes or until mixture thickens and coats a metal spoon. Remove from heat; cool. Stir in vanilla and yogurt. Freeze in ice cream maker according to manufacturer's directions; or follow refrigerator-freezer instructions on page 11. Sprinkle topping over each serving.

1 serving made with eggs contains:				
Cal	Carb	Fat	Chol	Calcium
225	45g	3g	108mg	149mg

1 serving made with egg substitute contains:				
Cal	Carb	Fat	Chol	Calcium
246	45g	1g	2mg	154mg

Chocolate, Coffee, and Tea

ICE CREAM
Country Chocolate Ice Cream

Old-Fashioned Chocolate Ice Cream

Fudge Ice Cream

Rocky Road Ice Cream

Peanut Butter-Fudge Ice Cream

Chocolate-Chip Mint Ice Cream

Fudge Ripple Ice Cream

White Chocolate Ice Cream

SHERBETS/SORBETS/ICES
Heavenly Chocolate Sherbet

Chocolate Frozen Yogurt

Sugar-Free Chocolate Frozen Yogurt

Chocolate-Marshmallow-Nut Frozen Yogurt

Chocolate Delight Frozen Yogurt

Chocolate Fleck Frozen Yogurt

Toasted Almond-Fudge Frozen Yogurt

Chocolate-Peanut Butter Frozen Yogurt

Sicilian Cheesecake Frozen Yogurt

COFFEE/TEA
Mocha-Bahia Frozen Yogurt

Café au Lait Ice Cream

Latté Frozen Yogurt

Irish-Coffee Ice Cream

Ginger-Tea Ice Cream

Iced Lemon-Orange Tea

Country Chocolate Ice Cream

COCOA POWDER DELIVERS GREAT FLAVOR TO THIS EASY-TO-MAKE TREAT. FOR ADDED FLAVOR, USE DUTCH IMPORTED COCOA.

Makes about 2 quarts

- ⅓ cup unsweetened cocoa powder
- 1½ cups sugar
- 1 (12-ounce) can evaporated milk
- 1 teaspoon vanilla extract
- 2 cups whipping cream

IN A MEDIUM SAUCEPAN, combine cocoa and sugar. Stir in evaporated milk. Stir over medium heat until cocoa and sugar dissolve; cool to room temperature. Add vanilla and whipping cream. Pour into ice cream canister. Freeze in ice cream maker according to manufacturer's directions; or follow refrigerator-freezer instructions on page 11.

1 serving contains:

Cal	Carb	Fat	Chol	Calcium
269	31g	16g	57mg	119mg

Old-Fashioned Chocolate Ice Cream

THIS IS SURE TO BECOME YOUR FAVORITE CHOCOLATE ICE CREAM, AS IT IS OURS.

Makes about 2 quarts

- 1⅓ cups sugar
- 1 tablespoon cornstarch
- ¼ teaspoon salt
- 3 cups milk
- 2 eggs
- 3 (1-ounce) squares semisweet chocolate, melted
- 1 (5-ounce) can evaporated milk
- 1 cup whipping cream
- 1 teaspoon vanilla extract

IN A MEDIUM SAUCEPAN, combine sugar, cornstarch, and salt. Stir in milk. Stir over medium heat until mixture begins to simmer. In a small bowl, beat eggs. Stir about 1 cup hot-milk mixture into beaten eggs. Stirring constantly, pour egg mixture into remaining hot-milk mixture. Cook and stir over low heat until slightly thickened, about 2 minutes. Add melted chocolate. Beat with a whisk until mixture is smooth. Stir in evaporated milk, whipping cream, and vanilla. Cool to room temperature. Pour into ice cream canister. Freeze in ice cream maker according to manufacturer's directions; or follow refrigerator-freezer instructions on page 11.

1 serving contains:

Cal	Carb	Fat	Chol	Calcium
254	31g	13g	72mg	131mg

Fudge Ice Cream

CHOCOHOLICS CAN'T RESIST THIS DARK AND EXTRA-RICH DESSERT!

Makes about 2 quarts

- 6 (1-ounce) squares unsweetened chocolate
- 2 tablespoons butter or margarine
- 2 cups sugar
- $\frac{1}{3}$ cup light corn syrup
- $\frac{2}{3}$ cup half-and-half
- 2 eggs
- 2 teaspoons vanilla extract
- $1\frac{1}{3}$ cups half-and-half
- 2 cups whipping cream

IN A MEDIUM SAUCEPAN, melt chocolate and butter or margarine over low heat, stirring often. Stir in sugar, corn syrup, and $\frac{2}{3}$ cup half-and-half. Stir over medium-low heat until mixture comes to a boil. Simmer 4 minutes without stirring; set aside. In a small bowl, beat eggs until blended. Stir in $\frac{1}{2}$ cup hot chocolate mixture. Stirring constantly, pour egg mixture into remaining chocolate mixture. Cook and stir over medium heat until slightly thickened, about 1 minute. Cool to lukewarm. Add vanilla, $1\frac{1}{3}$ cups half-and-half, and whipping cream. Pour into ice cream canister. Freeze in ice cream maker according to manufacturer's directions; or follow refrigerator-freezer instructions on page 11.

1 serving contains:

Cal	Carb	Fat	Chol	Calcium
443	50g	28g	110mg	82mg

Rocky Road Ice Cream

CHUNKY NUGGETS OF CHOCOLATE, NUTS, AND MARSHMALLOW WILL APPEAL TO CHOCOLATE LOVERS.

Makes about 2 quarts

- ⅓ cup unsweetened cocoa powder
- 1 cup sugar
- 2 cups milk
- 1 teaspoon vanilla extract
- ⅛ teaspoon salt
- 2 cups whipping cream
- 1 (1-ounce) square semisweet chocolate
- 1 cup miniature marshmallows
- ½ cup chopped almonds or pecans

IN A LARGE SAUCEPAN, mix cocoa powder and sugar. Gradually stir in milk. Stir over low heat until sugar and cocoa dissolve. Cool to room temperature. Add vanilla, salt, and whipping cream; set aside. Shred chocolate with coarse side of grater. Stir shredded chocolate, marshmallows, and almonds or pecans into cocoa mixture. Pour into ice cream canister. Freeze in ice cream maker according to manufacturer's directions; or follow refrigerator-freezer instructions on page 11.

1 serving contains:

Cal	Carb	Fat	Chol	Calcium
288	26g	20g	60mg	93mg

Peanut Butter-Fudge Ice Cream

HERE WE PAIRED TWO FAVORITE FLAVORS—YOU CAN'T MISS WITH THIS POPULAR COMBINATION.

Makes about 1½ quarts

- 1 (6-ounce) package semisweet chocolate pieces (1 cup)
- 2 cups milk
- 1 cup sugar
- ½ cup chunky peanut butter
- 1 teaspoon vanilla extract
- 2 cups half-and-half or whipping cream

IN A MEDIUM SAUCEPAN, combine chocolate pieces, milk, and sugar. Stir over low heat until chocolate melts. Stir in peanut butter. Cool to room temperature. Stir in vanilla and half-and-half or whipping cream. Pour into ice cream canister. Freeze in ice cream maker according to manufacturer's directions; or follow refrigerator-freezer instructions on page 11.

1 serving contains:

Cal	Carb	Fat	Chol	Calcium
328	35g	20g	24mg	124mg

Chocolate-Chip Mint Ice Cream

TINY CHOCOLATE FLECKS ARE SCATTERED THROUGHOUT THIS MINT-FLAVORED COMBINATION.

Makes about 1 quart

1½	cups half-and-half
3	tablespoons sugar
1	(3½-ounce) package instant vanilla-pudding mix
1	(12-ounce) can low-fat evaporated milk
1	(1-ounce) square semisweet chocolate, melted
⅓	cup finely chopped buttermints

IN MEDIUM BOWL, combine half-and-half, sugar, pudding mix, and evaporated milk. Slowly stir in melted chocolate so flecks of chocolate form. Stir in buttermints. Pour into ice cream canister. Freeze in ice cream maker according to manufacturer's directions; or follow refrigerator-freezer instructions on page 11.

1 serving contains:

Cal	Carb	Fat	Chol	Calcium
282	42g	10g	27mg	248mg

Fudge Ripple Ice Cream

FIRST MAKE THE FUDGE RIPPLE, THEN SWIRL IT THROUGH YOUR FAVORITE VANILLA ICE CREAM.

Makes about 2 quarts

FUDGE RIPPLE:

- ¼ cup sugar
- 2 tablespoons unsweetened cocoa powder
- ¼ cup light corn syrup
- 2 tablespoons half-and-half
- 1 tablespoon butter or margarine
- ¼ teaspoon vanilla extract
- 2 quarts Old-Fashioned Vanilla Ice Cream, page 16, made with 1 cup sugar

Fudge Ripple: In a small saucepan, combine sugar and cocoa powder. Stir in corn syrup and half-and-half. Stir occasionally over medium heat until mixture comes to a boil. Simmer 3 minutes, stirring occasionally. Add butter or margarine and vanilla. Set aside to cool.

Make Old-Fashioned Ice Cream, using only 1 cup sugar. When frozen, remove lid and dasher from ice cream canister. Insert a long spatula into center of ice cream. Pull spatula toward edge of canister. Quickly pour in cooled Fudge Ripple. Pull spatula through ice cream and sauce to create a marbled effect. Remove spatula. Cover canister with waxed paper or plastic wrap. Top with lid. Plug dasher hole with a cork or ball of foil. Ripen in brine, page 11, or place in freezer.

1 serving contains:

Cal	Carb	Fat	Chol	Calcium
153	24g	6g	44mg	102mg

White Chocolate Ice Cream

NOT QUITE AS PRONOUNCED IN FLAVOR AS THE DARK, WHITE CHOCOLATE HAS A DELICATE, MELLOW FLAVOR.

Makes about 1 quart

- 1 cup milk
- 2 tablespoons sugar
- 2 eggs, beaten
- 6 ounces coarsely chopped white chocolate or 1 cup white chocolate chips
- 1 cup half-and-half or whipping cream
- ½ teaspoon vanilla extract

IN MEDIUM SAUCEPAN, combine milk, sugar, and beaten eggs. Cook and stir over low heat until mixture thickens slightly. Remove from heat and add chocolate; stir until melted. Stir in half-and-half or whipping cream and vanilla. Cool. Pour into ice cream canister. Freeze in ice cream maker according to manufacturer's directions; or follow refrigerator-freezer instructions on page 11.

1 serving contains:

Cal	Carb	Fat	Chol	Calcium
272	25g	17g	97mg	155mg

Heavenly Chocolate Sherbet

A DELIGHTFUL CHOCOLATE FLAVOR WITH A PLEASING SHERBET TEXTURE.

Makes about 1 quart

- 1 (5.5-ounce) can chocolate-flavored syrup
- ½ cup sugar
- 2½ cups milk
- ½ teaspoon vanilla extract

IN A MEDIUM BOWL, combine chocolate-flavored syrup, sugar, milk, and vanilla. Stir until sugar dissolves. Pour into ice cream canister. Freeze in ice cream maker according to manufacturer's directions; or follow refrigerator-freezer instructions on page 11.

1 serving contains:

Cal	Carb	Fat	Chol	Calcium
222	43g	4g	14mg	127mg

Chocolate Frozen Yogurt

WHAT WOULD CHOCOLATE FANS DO WITHOUT CHOCOLATE SYRUP?

Makes about 1 quart

2 teaspoons cornstarch

½ cup sugar

1 (12-ounce) can evaporated skimmed or evaporated low-fat milk

1 egg, slightly beaten

⅔ cup chocolate syrup

½ teaspoon vanilla extract

1 cup plain low-fat yogurt, stirred

IN A MEDIUM SAUCEPAN, combine cornstarch and sugar. Stir in milk and egg. Cook and stir over low heat 6 to 8 minutes or until mixture coats a metal spoon. Remove from heat. Add chocolate syrup and cool. Stir in vanilla and yogurt. Freeze in ice cream maker according to manufacturer's directions; or follow refrigerator-freezer instructions on page 11.

1 serving contains:

Cal	Carb	Fat	Chol	Calcium
229	47g	2g	40mg	269mg

Sugar-Free Chocolate Frozen Yogurt

USING AN ARTIFICIAL SWEETENER ELIMINATES THE NEED FOR SUGAR IN THIS LOW-FAT TREAT.

Makes about 1 quart

½	cup low-fat milk
1	teaspoon unflavored gelatin
½	cup chocolate-flavored syrup
1	cup plain low-fat yogurt, stirred
4	(1-gram) packets Equal® sugar substitute
½	teaspoon vanilla extract
1	egg white
⅓	cup water
⅓	cup nonfat dry milk

IN A SMALL SAUCEPAN, combine ½ cup low-fat milk and gelatin; let stand 1 minute. Stir over low heat until gelatin dissolves; set aside. In small bowl, stir chocolate syrup into yogurt. Add Equal and vanilla. Stir in dissolved gelatin. In medium bowl, combine egg white, water, and nonfat dry milk. Beat until stiff peaks form. Fold into chocolate mixture. Freeze in ice cream maker according to manufacturer's directions; or follow refrigerator-freezer instructions on page 11.

1 serving contains:

Cal	Carb	Fat	Chol	Calcium
111	21g	1g	5mg	154mg

Chocolate-Marshmallow-Nut Frozen Yogurt

AN IRRESISTIBLE TEMPTATION OF CHOCOLATE YOGURT STUDDED WITH CHUNKS OF MARSHMALLOWS AND NUTS.

Makes about 1 quart

- ¼ cup unsweetened cocoa powder
- 2 teaspoons cornstarch
- ¾ cup sugar
- 1¼ cups low-fat milk
- 1½ cups plain low-fat yogurt, stirred
- ½ teaspoon vanilla extract
- ½ cup miniature marshmallows, halved
- ¼ cup chopped pecans or walnuts

IN A MEDIUM SAUCEPAN, combine cocoa powder, cornstarch, and sugar. Stir in milk. Cook and stir over moderate heat until mixture simmers and is slightly thickened. Remove from heat; cool. Stir in yogurt, vanilla, marshmallows, and nuts. Freeze in ice cream maker according to manufacturer's directions; or follow refrigerator-freezer instructions on page 11.

1 serving contains:

Cal	Carb	Fat	Chol	Calcium
218	39g	6g	8mg	181mg

Chocolate Delight Frozen Yogurt

HERE COCOA POWDER DELIVERS A DIVINE FLAVOR WE ALL LOVE.

Makes about 1 quart

¼	cup unsweetened cocoa powder
¾	cup sugar
1	(12-ounce) can evaporated skim or evaporated low-fat milk
1	(8-ounce) carton egg substitute (Egg Beaters®), thawed
½	teaspoon vanilla extract
1	cup plain yogurt, stirred

IN A MEDIUM SAUCEPAN, combine cocoa and sugar. Add milk and egg substitute. Whisk until smooth. Cook and whisk over moderate heat until mixture is very thick; cool. Stir in vanilla and yogurt. Freeze in ice cream maker according to manufacturer's directions; or follow refrigerator-freezer instructions on page 11.

1 serving contains:

Cal	Carb	Fat	Chol	Calcium
212	36g	3g	8mg	260mg

Chocolate Fleck Frozen Yogurt

WHEN MELTED CHOCOLATE CONTACTS COLD YOGURT, IT BREAKS INTO THIN CHIPS TO PROVIDE A GREAT FLAVOR.

Makes about 1 quart

- ¾ cup sugar
- 2 teaspoons cornstarch
- 1 (12-ounce) can evaporated low-fat milk
- 1 teaspoon vanilla extract
- 1 cup plain low-fat yogurt, stirred
- 2 ounces semisweet chocolate

IN A MEDIUM SAUCEPAN, combine sugar and cornstarch. Stir in milk. Cook and stir over moderate heat until thickened and bubbly. Remove from heat; cool to lukewarm. Add vanilla and yogurt. Refrigerate until mixture is cold. Melt chocolate. While chocolate is hot, pour it very slowly into chilled yogurt mixture while stirring gently. Freeze in ice cream maker according to manufacturer's directions; or follow refrigerator-freezer instructions on page 11.

1 serving contains:

Cal	Carb	Fat	Chol	Calcium
207	41g	3g	8mg	266mg

Toasted Almond-Fudge Frozen Yogurt

TOAST BLANCHED ALMONDS IN A 375F (190C) OVEN FOR 6 TO 8 MINUTES OR UNTIL LIGHT TAN; COOL BEFORE USING.

Makes about 1 quart

¾ cup granulated sugar	1 teaspoon vanilla extract
3 tablespoons unsweetened cocoa powder	½ cup coarsely chopped, toasted, blanched almonds
¼ teaspoon salt, optional	⅓ cup fat-free milk
1¼ cups fat-free milk	1 tablespoon fat-free dry milk
1 tablespoon light corn syrup	1 tablespoon powdered sugar
1 tablespoon margarine or butter, optional	1¼ cups plain fat-free yogurt, stirred

IN A 1½-QUART SAUCEPAN, combine granulated sugar, cocoa powder, salt (if desired), 1¼ cups fat-free milk, and corn syrup. Add margarine or butter, if desired. Simmer over medium-low heat, stirring frequently for 8 to 10 minutes. Remove from heat; stir in vanilla and toasted almonds. Cool. In bowl, combine ⅓ cup fat-free milk and fat-free dry milk; stir until dry milk dissolves. Place beater in bowl with milk. Freeze in refrigerator-freezer until ice crystals form around edge of milk (about 30 minutes). Remove mixer bowl and beaters from freezer; beat with electric mixer on medium speed until soft peaks form. Add powdered sugar and continue beating on high speed until stiff peaks form. Stir yogurt into cooled cocoa mixture. Fold in whipped milk. Freeze in ice cream maker according to manufacturer's directions; or follow refrigerator-freezer instructions on page 11.

1 serving contains:

Cal	Carb	Fat	Chol	Calcium
229	40g	6g	2mg	187mg

Chocolate-Peanut Butter Frozen Yogurt

A MAGICAL, MOUTH-WATERING COMBINATION OF NOSTALGIC FAVORITES THAT GO TOGETHER BEAUTIFULLY.

Makes about 1 quart

- ¼ cup crunchy peanut butter
- 2 ounces semisweet chocolate, melted
- 1 medium banana, peeled and mashed
- 1 (12-ounce) can evaporated low-fat milk
- ½ cup sugar
- ½ teaspoon vanilla extract
- 1 cup plain low-fat yogurt, stirred

IN A MEDIUM BOWL, combine peanut butter, melted chocolate, and banana. Add evaporated milk, sugar, and vanilla. Stir in yogurt. Freeze in ice cream maker according to manufacturer's directions; or follow refrigerator-freezer instructions on page 11.

1 serving contains:

Cal	Carb	Fat	Chol	Calcium
275	38g	11g	8mg	265mg

Sicilian Cheesecake Frozen Yogurt

WE BORROWED MEDITERRANEAN FLAVOR COMBINATIONS FOR THIS UNUSUAL DESSERT.

Makes about 1 quart

- 3 ounces semisweet chocolate, coarsely chopped
- 2 eggs, slightly beaten
- ⅔ cup low-fat milk
- ¾ cup cottage cheese
- ½ cup sugar
- 1 tablespoon rum or rum flavoring
- 1 cup plain low-fat yogurt, stirred
- ⅓ cup chopped candied fruits

IN A MEDIUM SAUCEPAN, combine chocolate, eggs, and milk. Cook and stir over low heat until chocolate melts; remove from heat. In blender or food processor fitted with metal blade, purée cottage cheese and sugar. Add to chocolate mixture; stir until smooth. Cool; then add rum, yogurt, and fruits. Freeze in ice cream maker according to manufacturer's directions; or follow refrigerator-freezer instructions on page 11.

1 serving contains:

Cal	Carb	Fat	Chol	Calcium
245	31g	10g	80mg	243mg

Mocha-Bahia Frozen Yogurt

CHOCOLATE, CINNAMON, AND COFFEE ARE TEAMED TO PRODUCE A TRIPLE-FLAVOR TREAT.

Makes about 1 quart

- 2 tablespoons water
- 1 teaspoon unflavored gelatin
- 3 ounces semisweet chocolate, coarsely chopped
- 1½ cups low-fat milk
- ¼ teaspoon ground cinnamon
- 2 teaspoons instant-coffee crystals
- ¾ cup sugar
- 1 cup plain low-fat yogurt, stirred

IN A MEASURING CUP, combine water and gelatin; set aside. In medium saucepan, combine chocolate, milk, cinnamon, coffee crystals, and sugar. Cook and stir over medium-low heat until chocolate melts. Remove from heat; stir in softened gelatin. Cool; then add yogurt. Freeze in ice cream maker according to manufacturer's directions; or follow refrigerator-freezer instructions on page 11.

1 serving contains:

Cal	Carb	Fat	Chol	Calcium
224	38g	7g	7mg	160mg

Café au Lait Ice Cream

ACHIEVE SIMPLY ELEGANT RESULTS WHEN YOU COMBINE COFFEE AND MILK THE FRENCH WAY.

Makes about 1 quart

- 2 eggs, beaten
- ⅔ cup sugar
- 1½ cups milk
- 2 tablespoons instant-coffee crystals
- ½ teaspoon vanilla extract
- ¼ cup miniature marshmallows
- 1 cup half-and-half or whipping cream

IN A MEDIUM SAUCEPAN, combine beaten eggs, sugar, and milk. Cook and stir over low heat until mixture thickens and coats a spoon. Add coffee crystals; stir in vanilla and marshmallows until melted. Set aside to cool 15 minutes. Add half-and-half or whipping cream. Pour into ice cream canister. Freeze in ice cream maker according to manufacturer's directions; or follow refrigerator-freezer instructions on page 11.

1 serving contains:

Cal	Carb	Fat	Chol	Calcium
205	29g	7g	90mg	128mg

Latté Frozen Yogurt

FROZEN COFFEE AND CREAM, PERFECT AFTER ANY SPECIAL MEAL.

| Makes about 1 quart |

- ²⁄₃ **cup sugar**
- 2 **teaspoons cornstarch**
- 1¼ **cups low-fat milk**
- 1 **tablespoon instant-coffee crystals**
- 1 **egg**
- ¼ **cup miniature or cut-up large marshmallows**
- ½ **teaspoon vanilla extract**
- 1½ **cups plain low-fat yogurt, stirred**

IN A 1½- OR 2-QUART SAUCEPAN, combine sugar and cornstarch. Stir in milk and instant-coffee. Cook and stir over medium heat until mixture simmers. In small bowl, beat egg slightly; stir about ½ cup hot mixture into beaten egg. Pour egg mixture into pan with remaining hot liquid. Cook and stir over low heat until slightly thickened. Remove from heat; add marshmallows and stir until dissolved. Cool. Stir in vanilla and yogurt. Freeze in ice cream maker according to manufacturer's directions; or follow refrigerator-freezer instructions on page 11.

1 serving contains:

Cal	Carb	Fat	Chol	Calcium
175	32g	3g	43mg	180mg

Irish-Coffee Ice Cream

CELEBRATE ST. PATRICK'S DAY OR ANY DAY WITH THIS SPECIAL DESSERT.

Makes about 2 quarts

- 2 **eggs, beaten**
- 2 **cups milk**
- 1 **cup firmly packed brown sugar**
- 4 **tablespoons instant-coffee crystals**
- ½ **cup Irish whiskey or brandy**
- 2 **teaspoons vanilla extract**
- 2 **cups half-and-half or whipping cream**

IN A MEDIUM SAUCEPAN, combine beaten eggs, milk, brown sugar, and instant-coffee crystals. Cook and stir over medium-low heat until sugar and coffee dissolve and mixture thickens slightly. Remove from heat; stir in whiskey or brandy. Cool to room temperature. Stir in vanilla and half-and-half or whipping cream. Pour into ice cream canister. Freeze in ice cream maker according to manufacturer's directions; or follow refrigerator-freezer instructions on page 11.

1 serving contains:

Cal	Carb	Fat	Chol	Calcium
184	22g	6g	53mg	114mg

Ginger-Tea Ice Cream

IMPRESS YOUR GUESTS WITH AN UNBELIEVABLY SMOOTH, GINGER-ACCENTED DESSERT.

Makes about 1 quart

- **4 egg yolks**
- **½ cup sugar**
- **2 cups half-and-half**
- **1 tablespoon instant-tea powder**
- **2 tablespoons finely chopped crystallized ginger**
- **¾ cup whipping cream**

IN A LARGE BOWL, beat egg yolks and sugar until well blended. Stir in half-and-half, tea powder, and ginger. Pour into a medium saucepan. Cook and stir over low heat until slightly thickened. Cool slightly; add whipping cream. Pour into ice cream canister. Freeze in ice cream maker according to manufacturer's directions; or follow refrigerator-freezer instructions on page 11.

1 serving contains:

Cal	Carb	Fat	Chol	Calcium
329	25g	24g	212mg	130mg

Iced Lemon-Orange Tea

IDEAL FOR A WARM DAY! RELAX AND SAVOR A REFRESHING ICED CONFECTION.

Makes about 2 quarts

6 cups water

1 cup honey

2 teaspoons grated fresh orange peel

6 tea bags

¼ cup lemon juice

IN A LARGE SAUCEPAN, combine water, honey, and orange peel. Stir over medium heat until mixture comes to a boil; remove from heat. Add tea bags. Cover and steep 5 minutes. Remove tea bags; cool syrup to room temperature. Stir in lemon juice. Pour into ice cream canister. Freeze in ice cream maker according to manufacturer's directions; or follow refrigerator-freezer instructions on page 11.

1 serving contains:

Cal	Carb	Fat	Chol	Calcium
87	24g	0g	0mg	5mg

Berries and Fruits of the Vine

STRAWBERRY
Fresh Strawberry Ice Cream
Quick-and-Easy Strawberry
  Ice Cream
Strawberry Ice Cream
Strawberry Sherbet
Strawberry-Orange Sorbet
Strawberry-Rhubarb Sorbet
Strawberry Frozen Yogurt
Strawberry-Banana Frozen Yogurt
Strawberry-Cream Frozen Yogurt

RASPBERRY
Fresh Raspberry Ice Cream
Tangy Raspberry Ice Cream
Favorite Raspberry Frozen Yogurt
Crimson Berry Frozen Yogurt
Raspberry-Marshmallow Yogurt
Sugar-Free Raspberry Frozen Yogurt

BLACKBERRY
Blackberry Frozen Yogurt

Crunchy Blackberry Frozen Yogurt
Blackberry-White Chocolate
  Swirl Frozen Yogurt

BOYSENBERRY
Boysenberry Sherbet
Boysenberry Supreme Frozen
  Yogurt
Boysenberry-Cassis Frozen Yogurt

BLUEBERRY
Blueberry-Orange Ice Cream
Blueberry Sorbet
Blueberry-Marshmallow Frozen
  Yogurt

CRANBERRY
Cranberry-Orange Sherbet
Cranberry-Wine Sorbet

WATERMELON
Watermelon-Berry Sorbet

Fresh Strawberry Ice Cream

WELCOME SUMMER WITH FRESH STRAWBERRIES CHURNED INTO A COLORFUL DESSERT.

Makes about 1 quart

- ½ cup sugar
- 2 teaspoons cornstarch
- 1 cup half-and-half
- 2 eggs, beaten
- 2 tablespoons light corn syrup
- 2 cups fresh or frozen strawberries, thawed
- ½ cup whipping cream

IN A SMALL SAUCEPAN, combine sugar and cornstarch. Stir in half-and-half. Cook and stir over medium heat until mixture simmers. Cook 1 minute longer. Remove from heat. Slowly stir half of hot mixture into beaten eggs. Stirring constantly, pour egg mixture into remaining hot mixture; return pan to heat. Cook and stir over low heat about 2 minutes or until mixture thickens. Stir in corn syrup; cool. In blender or food processor fitted with metal blade, process strawberries until almost smooth. Add strawberries and whipping cream to egg mixture. Pour into ice cream canister. Freeze in ice cream maker according to manufacturer's directions; or follow refrigerator-freezer instructions on page 11.

1 serving contains:

Cal	Carb	Fat	Chol	Calcium
248	29g	14g	113mg	71mg

Quick-and-Easy Strawberry Ice Cream

NO COOKING REQUIRED! MIX INGREDIENTS IN MINUTES AND FREEZE.

Makes about 1 quart

2	cups fresh or frozen unsweetened strawberries, thawed
½	cup sugar
1	tablespoon lemon juice
1	(14-ounce) can sweetened condensed milk
1	cup milk
2 to 4	drops red food coloring, if desired

PURÉE BERRIES in blender or food processor fitted with metal blade. In a large bowl, combine puréed berries, sugar, lemon juice, sweetened condensed milk, milk, and food coloring, if desired. Pour into ice cream canister. Freeze in ice cream maker according to manufacturer's directions; or follow refrigerator-freezer instructions on page 11.

1 serving contains:

Cal	Carb	Fat	Chol	Calcium
392	71g	9g	36mg	309mg

Strawberry Ice Cream

FOR THAT SPECIAL OCCASION, SERVE THIS VELVET-SMOOTH ICE CREAM. THIS RECIPE FEATURES THE WELCOME TANG OF DAIRY SOUR CREAM.

Makes about 1 quart

- 2 cups fresh or frozen strawberries, thawed
- 1 egg, beaten
- ½ cup sugar
- ½ cup half-and-half
- 1 cup dairy sour cream
- ½ teaspoon vanilla extract

PURÉE BERRIES in blender or food processor fitted with metal blade; set aside. In small saucepan, combine beaten egg, sugar, and half-and-half. Cook and stir over low heat until thickened. Cool slightly. Stir in puréed berries, sour cream, and vanilla. Pour into ice cream canister. Freeze in ice cream maker according to manufacturer's directions; or follow refrigerator-freezer instructions on page 11.

1 serving contains:

Cal	Carb	Fat	Chol	Calcium
201	23g	11g	60mg	77mg

Strawberry Sherbet

THE TEXTURE OF THIS SHERBET IS SMOOTHER THAN EXPECTED DUE TO THE ADDITION OF GELATIN.

Makes about 2 quarts

1	teaspoon unflavored gelatin
2	tablespoons lemon juice
2	cups milk
1½	cups sugar
4	cups fresh or frozen unsweetened strawberries, thawed

IN A SMALL BOWL, sprinkle gelatin over lemon juice; set aside for 1 minute. In a medium saucepan, combine milk and sugar. Stir over low heat until sugar dissolves. Add softened gelatin; set aside. Purée berries in blender or food processor fitted with metal blade. Stir into milk mixture. Cool to room temperature. Pour into ice cream canister. Freeze in ice cream maker according to manufacturer's directions; or follow refrigerator-freezer instructions on page 11.

1 serving contains:

Cal	Carb	Fat	Chol	Calcium
138	31g	2g	6mg	56mg

Strawberry-Orange Sorbet

FOR THE BEST FLAVOR, USE THOROUGHLY RIPENED STRAWBERRIES AND FRESH ORANGE JUICE, IF POSSIBLE.

Makes about 1 quart

1	cup water
¾	cup sugar
2	cups fresh strawberries
½	cup orange juice

IN A SMALL SAUCEPAN, combine water and sugar. Stir over low heat until sugar dissolves; bring to a boil. Boil gently 5 minutes without stiffing; set aside to cool. Wash strawberries; remove and discard caps. Purée strawberries in blender or food processor fitted with metal blade. In a medium bowl, combine puréed strawberries, cooled syrup, and orange juice. Pour into ice cream canister. Freeze in ice cream maker according to manufacturer's directions; or follow refrigerator freezer instructions on page 11.

1 serving contains:

Cal	Carb	Fat	Chol	Calcium
121	31g	0g	0mg	10mg

Strawberry-Rhubarb Sorbet

PERHAPS YOU'VE NEVER IMAGINED RHUBARB IN ICE CREAM, BUT YOU'LL CHANGE YOUR MIND AFTER TASTING THIS FROSTY VERSION OF A WELL-LOVED FLAVOR COMBINATION.

Makes about 1 quart

1	pound fresh rhubarb, cut in 1-inch pieces (4 cups)
¼	cup water
1½	cups sugar
2	cups fresh or frozen unsweetened strawberries, thawed

IN A MEDIUM SAUCEPAN, combine rhubarb and water. Bring to a boil over medium heat. Cover and simmer until rhubarb is tender, about 5 minutes. Stir in sugar until dissolved. Purée rhubarb mixture in blender or food processor fitted with metal blade. Pour into a large bowl; set aside. Purée strawberries in blender or food processor fitted with metal blade. Stir into rhubarb mixture. Pour into ice cream canister. Freeze in ice cream maker according to manufacturer's directions; or follow refrigerator-freezer instructions on page 11.

1 serving contains:

Cal	Carb	Fat	Chol	Calcium
225	57g	0g	0mg	73mg

Strawberry Frozen Yogurt

WE PROVE FAT-FREE CAN BE DELICIOUS. PROUDLY SERVE THIS VERY SMOOTH, CREAMY DESSERT, WHICH IS LOW IN FAT AND CHOLESTEROL.

Makes about 1 quart

- ¼ cup fat-free milk
- 2 tablespoons fat-free dry milk
- 1 tablespoon sugar
- 1 teaspoon unflavored gelatin
- ⅔ cup fat-free milk
- 1 cup fresh or frozen unsweetened strawberries
- ⅔ cup sugar
- ½ teaspoon vanilla extract
- 1 cup plain fat-free yogurt, stirred

IN A SMALL MIXER BOWL, combine ¼ cup fat-free milk with fat-free dry milk; stir until dry milk dissolves. Place mixer bowl and beaters in refrigerator-freezer until ice crystals begin to form around edge of milk (about 30 minutes). Remove mixer bowl and beaters from freezer; beat at high speed until soft peaks form. Continue beating while adding 1 tablespoon sugar until stiff peaks form; refrigerate. In small saucepan, sprinkle gelatin over ⅔ cup milk; let stand 1 minute. Cook and stir over very low heat just until gelatin dissolves. Remove from heat; set aside. In blender or food processor, purée strawberries with ⅔ cup sugar until sugar dissolves. In medium bowl, combine strawberry purée, gelatin mixture, vanilla extract, and yogurt. Fold whipped milk into strawberry mixture. Freeze in ice cream maker according to manufacturer's directions; or follow refrigerator-freezer instructions on page 11.

1 serving contains:

Cal	Carb	Fat	Chol	Calcium
139	32g	0g	2mg	119mg

Strawberry-Banana Frozen Yogurt

THE BANANA CONTRIBUTES A SURPRISINGLY SMOOTH TEXTURE.

Makes about 1 quart

½	cup low-fat milk
1	egg, slightly beaten
1½	cups fresh or frozen unsweetened strawberries
1	small banana, peeled and quartered
2	tablespoons light corn syrup
½	cup brown sugar
¼	teaspoon vanilla extract
¾	cup plain low-fat yogurt, stirred

IN A SMALL SAUCEPAN, cook and stir milk and egg over low heat until thickened; set aside. In blender or food processor fitted with metal blade, combine strawberries, banana, corn syrup, brown sugar, and vanilla. Process until finely chopped. Combine with cooked egg mixture. Stir in yogurt. Freeze in ice cream maker according to manufacturer's directions; or follow refrigerator-freezer instructions on page 11.

1 serving contains:

Cal	Carb	Fat	Chol	Calcium
157	33g	2g	39mg	107mg

Strawberry-Cream Frozen Yogurt

INDULGE YOURSELF OCCASIONALLY AND ENJOY THIS RICH TREAT.

Makes about 1 quart

- ½ cup sugar
- 2 teaspoons cornstarch
- 1 cup half-and-half or whipping cream
- ¼ cup light corn syrup
- 1 egg, slightly beaten
- 2 cups fresh or frozen unsweetened strawberries
- 1 cup plain low-fat yogurt, stirred

IN A MEDIUM SAUCEPAN, combine sugar and cornstarch; stir in half-and-half and corn syrup. Cook and stir over moderate heat until mixture simmers; cook 1 minute longer. Remove from heat; stir in beaten egg. Return to low heat; cook and stir 2 minutes. Remove from heat; cool. In blender or food processor fitted with metal blade, purée berries. Add to cool egg mixture; stir in yogurt. Freeze in ice cream maker according to manufacturer's directions; or follow refrigerator-freezer instructions on page 11.

1 serving contains:

Cal	Carb	Fat	Chol	Calcium
212	36g	6g	53mg	129mg

Fresh Raspberry Ice Cream

NOTHING ELSE COMPARES TO FRESH RASPBERRY FLAVOR.

Makes about 1 quart

- 2 cups fresh or frozen raspberries, thawed
- 1 egg, beaten
- ½ cup sugar
- 2 tablespoons light corn syrup
- 1 (12-ounce) can evaporated low-fat milk
- 1 cup half-and-half

IN BLENDER OR FOOD PROCESSOR fitted with metal blade, purée raspberries. Strain and discard seeds. Set purée aside. In small saucepan, combine beaten egg, sugar, corn syrup, and evaporated milk. Cook and stir over low heat until thickened; cool. Combine with raspberry purée and half-and-half. Pour into ice cream canister. Freeze in ice cream maker according to manufacturer's directions; or follow refrigerator-freezer instructions on page 11.

1 serving contains:

Cal	Carb	Fat	Chol	Calcium
227	36g	7g	55mg	235mg

Tangy Raspberry Ice Cream

BUTTERMILK BLENDED WITH RASPBERRIES PROVIDES A PLEASING TANG.

Makes about 1 quart

- ²⁄₃ cup sugar
- 2 teaspoons cornstarch
- 1 (12-ounce) can evaporated low-fat milk
- 2 tablespoons light corn syrup
- 1 egg, beaten
- 2 cups fresh or frozen unsweetened raspberries, thawed
- 1 cup buttermilk

IN A MEDIUM SAUCEPAN, combine sugar and cornstarch. Stir in evaporated milk and corn syrup. Cook and stir over medium heat until mixture is bubbly; remove from heat. Stir half of hot-milk mixture into beaten egg. Stirring constantly, pour egg mixture into remaining hot-milk mixture. Return mixture to saucepan; cook and stir over low heat until mixture coats a spoon and is slightly thickened. Set aside to cool. In blender or food processor fitted with metal blade, purée berries. Strain and discard seeds. Add berry juice to cooked mixture; stir in buttermilk. Pour into ice cream canister. Freeze in ice cream maker according to manufacturer's directions; or follow refrigerator-freezer instructions on page 11.

1 serving contains:

Cal	Carb	Fat	Chol	Calcium
216	42g	3g	42mg	240mg

Favorite Raspberry Frozen Yogurt

A TOUCH OF HONEY DOES WONDERS FOR FRESH RASPBERRIES.

Makes about 1 quart

- 2 cups fresh or frozen unsweetened raspberries
- ⅔ cup sugar
- 2 teaspoons cornstarch
- ¼ cup honey
- 1 cup low-fat milk
- 1 cup plain low-fat yogurt, stirred

IN A BLENDER OR FOOD PROCESSOR fitted with metal blade, purée raspberries; strain and discard seeds. In medium saucepan, mix sugar and cornstarch. Stir in honey and milk. Cook and stir over low heat until mixture simmers (about 6 to 8 minutes). Remove from heat; add puréed berries. Cool; stir in yogurt. Freeze in ice cream maker according to manufacturer's directions; or follow refrigerator-freezer instructions on page 11.

1 serving contains:

Cal	Carb	Fat	Chol	Calcium
198	44g	2g	6mg	134mg

Crimson Berry Frozen Yogurt

SERVE THIS BEAUTIFUL, RICH-TASTING DESSERT TOPPED WITH A DOLLOP OF WHIPPED CREAM.

Makes about 1 quart

1	cup low-fat milk
½	cup sugar
3	tablespoons light corn syrup
1	(8-ounce) carton egg substitute (such as Egg Beaters®), thawed
2	cups fresh or frozen unsweetened raspberries
1	cup plain low-fat yogurt, stirred

IN A MEDIUM SAUCEPAN, combine milk, sugar, and corn syrup. Stir in egg substitute; whisk until smooth. Cook and stir over moderate heat until mixture is very thick; remove from heat. In blender or food processor fitted with metal blade, purée berries; strain and discard seeds. Stir strained berries and yogurt into cooked mixture. Freeze in ice cream maker according to manufacturer's directions; or follow refrigerator-freezer instructions on page 11.

1 serving contains:

Cal	Carb	Fat	Chol	Calcium
195	34g	3g	6mg	156mg

Raspberry-Marshmallow Frozen Yogurt

AN UNUSUAL COMBINATION THAT WORKS VERY WELL TOGETHER.

Makes about 1 quart

- 1 cup fresh or frozen unsweetened raspberries
- 1 teaspoon unflavored gelatin
- ¼ cup water
- 1 cup unsweetened applesauce
- ⅔ cup sugar
- ½ cup miniature marshmallows, halved
- 1 cup plain low-fat yogurt, stirred

IN A BLENDER OR FOOD PROCESSOR fitted with metal blade, purée raspberries. Strain and discard seeds. In a small saucepan, combine gelatin and water; let stand 1 minute. Cook and stir over low heat until gelatin dissolves. Combine with puréed raspberries, applesauce, sugar, and marshmallows. Stir in yogurt. Cover; refrigerate at least ½ hour before freezing. Freeze in ice cream maker according to manufacturer's directions; or follow refrigerator-freezer instructions on page 11.

1 serving contains:

Cal	Carb	Fat	Chol	Calcium
153	35g	1g	2mg	81mg

Sugar-Free Raspberry Frozen Yogurt

ENJOY THIS GREAT DESSERT WITHOUT WORRYING ABOUT THE SUGAR CONTENT.

Makes about 1 quart

- ¼ cup water
- 1 teaspoon unflavored gelatin
- 1 cup fresh or frozen unsweetened raspberries
- 12 (1-gram) packets Equal® sugar substitute
- 1 cup plain low-fat yogurt, stirred
- 1 egg white
- ⅓ cup cold water
- ⅓ cup fat-free dry milk

IN A SMALL SAUCEPAN, combine ¼ cup water with gelatin; let stand 1 minute. Cook and stir over low heat until gelatin dissolves; set aside. In blender or food processor fitted with metal blade, purée berries. Strain; discard seeds. Combine puréed berries with Equal® and dissolved gelatin. Stir in yogurt. In a small bowl, combine egg white with ⅓ cup water, and dry milk; beat until stiff but not dry. Fold into raspberry mixture. Freeze in ice cream maker according to manufacturer's directions; or follow refrigerator-freezer instructions on page 11.

1 serving contains:

Cal	Carb	Fat	Chol	Calcium
61	7g	1g	3mg	131mg

Blackberry Frozen Yogurt

LUCKY IS THE PERSON WHO CAN ENJOY THE FRUITS OF HIS OR HER OWN BERRY CROP!

Makes about 1 quart

- 2 cups fresh or frozen unsweetened blackberries or boysenberries
- 2/3 cup sugar
- 2 teaspoons cornstarch
- 2 tablespoons honey
- 1 cup low-fat milk
- 1 cup plain low-fat yogurt, stirred

IN A BLENDER OR FOOD PROCESSOR fitted with metal blade, purée berries; strain and discard seeds. Set purée aside. In small saucepan, combine sugar and cornstarch. Stir in honey and milk. Cook and stir over medium heat until translucent (about 5 to 7 minutes). Stir in puréed berries. Cool; then add yogurt. Freeze in ice cream maker according to manufacturer's directions; or follow refrigerator-freezer instructions on page 11.

1 serving contains:

Cal	Carb	Fat	Chol	Calcium
182	40g	2g	6mg	140mg

Crunchy Blackberry Frozen Yogurt

TOP A FRESH FRUIT SALAD WITH A SCOOP OF THIS! STIR IN THE GRANOLA AFTER BERRY MIXTURE IS FROZEN SO YOU'LL HAVE A CONTRAST OF CRUNCHY AND SMOOTH TEXTURES.

Makes about 1 quart

- 2 cups fresh or frozen unsweetened blackberries or boysenberries
- 1 teaspoon unflavored gelatin
- ¼ cup water
- ⅔ cup sugar
- ¼ cup honey
- ½ cup apple juice
- 1 cup plain low-fat yogurt, stirred
- ½ cup granola

IN A BLENDER OR FOOD PROCESSOR fitted with metal blade, purée berries; strain and discard seeds. In small saucepan, sprinkle gelatin over water; let stand 1 minute. Cook and stir over low heat until gelatin dissolves. Combine with sugar, honey, apple juice, puréed berries, and yogurt. Freeze in ice cream maker according to manufacturer's directions. When frozen, stir in granola. Or follow refrigerator-freezer instructions on page 11 and stir in granola fter the final processing or beating.

1 serving contains:

Cal	Carb	Fat	Chol	Calcium
238	51g	3g	2mg	101mg

Blackberry-White Chocolate Swirl Frozen Yogurt

MAKE THIN STRIPS OF CHOCOLATE BY USING A SWIVEL-BLADE VEGETABLE PEELER OR THE COARSE SIDE OF A SHREDDER.

Makes about 1 quart

- 2 cups fresh or frozen unsweetened blackberries or boysenberries
- 1 teaspoon unflavored gelatin
- ¼ cup water
- ⅔ cup sugar
- ⅔ cup low-fat milk
- 1 cup plain low-fat yogurt, stirred
- 4 ounces white baking bar or white chocolate candy bar, coarsely shredded

IN A BLENDER OR FOOD PROCESSOR fitted with metal blade, purée berries. Strain and discard seeds; set purée aside. In a small saucepan, sprinkle gelatin over water; let stand 1 minute. Cook and stir over low heat until gelatin dissolves. Stir in sugar, milk, puréed berries, and yogurt. Then fold in shredded white chocolate. Freeze in ice cream maker according to manufacturer's directions; or follow refrigerator-freezer instructions on page 11.

1 serving contains:

Cal	Carb	Fat	Chol	Calcium
253	44g	7g	8mg	161mg

Boysenberry Sherbet

**BERRIES ADD WONDERFUL COLOR TO YOUR DESSERT. YOUR GUESTS WILL
NEVER KNOW THAT IT'S ACTUALLY SUGAR-FREE.**

Makes about 1 quart

1	teaspoon unflavored gelatin
2	tablespoons low-fat milk
2	cups fresh or frozen boysenberries or blackberries, thawed
12	(1-gram) packets Equal® sugar substitute
1	(12-ounce) can low-fat evaporated milk

IN SMALL SAUCEPAN, sprinkle gelatin on milk; let stand 1 minute. Stir over low heat until gelatin dissolves. Remove from heat. In blender or food processor fitted with metal blade, purée berries. Pour purée into a fine strainer. Use the back of a spoon to press purée through strainer into a small bowl; discard seeds. Combine puréed berries, sugar substitute, evaporated milk, and gelatin mixture. Pour into ice cream canister. Freeze in ice cream maker according to manufacturer's directions; or follow refrigerator-freezer instructions on page 11.

1 serving contains:

Cal	Carb	Fat	Chol	Calcium
303	13g	2g	5mg	202mg

Boysenberry Supreme Frozen Yogurt

CREAMY YET LIGHT-TEXTURED, WITH A REFRESHING, INTENSE BERRY FLAVOR, THIS DESSERT WILL BECOME ONE OF YOUR FAVORITES.

Makes about 1 quart

- ²/₃ cup sugar
- 2 teaspoons cornstarch
- ¾ cup evaporated skim milk
- 1 egg, slightly beaten
- 2 tablespoons light corn syrup
- 2 cups fresh or frozen unsweetened boysenberries
- 1 cup plain low-fat yogurt, stirred

IN A MEDIUM SAUCEPAN, combine sugar and cornstarch. Stir in milk, beaten egg, and corn syrup. Cook and stir over low heat until mixture coats metal spoon and is slightly thickened; set aside. In a blender or food processor fitted with metal blade, purée berries. Strain and discard seeds. Add to cooked mixture. Stir in yogurt. Freeze in ice cream maker according to manufacturer's directions; or follow refrigerator-freezer instructions on page 11.

1 serving contains:

Cal	Carb	Fat	Chol	Calcium
197	41g	2g	39mg	187mg

Boysenberry-Cassis Frozen Yogurt

IF FROZEN BERRIES ARE USED, THAW THEM BEFORE PURÉEING.

Makes about 1 quart

- 2 cups fresh or frozen unsweetened boysenberries or blackberries
- 1 teaspoon unflavored gelatin
- ½ cup low-fat milk
- ⅓ cup sugar
- 3 tablespoons Cassis (black-currant liqueur)
- ¼ cup light corn syrup
- 1½ cups plain low-fat yogurt, stirred

IN A BLENDER OR FOOD PROCESSOR fitted with metal blade, purée berries; strain and discard seeds. Set aside berry purée. In medium saucepan, sprinkle gelatin over milk; let stand 1 minute. Cook and stir over low heat until gelatin dissolves. Add sugar, Cassis, corn syrup, and puréed berries; cool. Stir in yogurt. Freeze in ice cream maker according to manufacturer's directions; or follow refrigerator-freezer instructions on page 11.

1 serving contains:

Cal	Carb	Fat	Chol	Calcium
183	36g	2g	5mg	153mg

Blueberry-Orange Ice Cream

ORANGE JUICE SEEMS TO HEIGHTEN THE FLAVOR OF THE BERRIES, AS WELL AS CONTRIBUTE TO THE SMOOTHNESS OF THIS ICE CREAM.

Makes about 1 quart

- ⅓ cup sugar
- 2 teaspoons cornstarch
- ¾ cup evaporated low-fat milk
- 1 egg, beaten
- 2 tablespoons light corn syrup
- 1 cup fresh or frozen blueberries, thawed
- ½ cup orange juice
- 1 cup half-and-half or whipping cream

IN MEDIUM SAUCEPAN, combine sugar and cornstarch. Stir in evaporated milk, beaten egg, and corn syrup. Cook and stir over low heat until mixture coats a spoon and is thickened; cool. In blender or food processor fitted with metal blade, purée berries with orange juice. Combine cooked mixture, puréed berries, and half-and-half or whipping cream. Pour into ice cream canister. Freeze in ice cream maker according to manufacturer's directions; or follow refrigerator-freezer instructions on page 11.

1 serving contains:

Cal	Carb	Fat	Chol	Calcium
183	28g	6g	58mg	137mg

Blueberry Sorbet

FOR A PATRIOTIC PRESENTATION, GARNISH EACH SERVING WITH A FAN-SLICED FRESH STRAWBERRY AND A DOLLOP OF WHIPPED CREAM.

Makes about 1½ quarts

1	cup sugar
½	cup light corn syrup
1	cup water
4	cups fresh or frozen blueberries, thawed
¼	cup lemon juice

IN A SMALL SAUCEPAN, combine sugar, corn syrup, and water. Stir over low heat until sugar dissolves; set aside. Purée blueberries in blender or food processor fitted with a metal blade. If desired, pour into a fine strainer. Use the back of a spoon to press purée through strainer into a small bowl. In a medium bowl, combine puréed blueberries, lemon juice, and syrup. Cool to room temperature. Pour into ice cream canister. Freeze in ice cream maker according to manufacturer's directions; or follow refrigerator-freezer instructions on page 11.

1 serving contains:

Cal	Carb	Fat	Chol	Calcium
175	46g	0g	0mg	6mg

Blueberry-Marshmallow Frozen Yogurt

MINIATURE MARSHMALLOWS CONTRIBUTE SURPRISING CONTRASTS OF COLOR, TEXTURE, AND FLAVOR.

Makes about 1 quart

- 2 cups fresh or unsweetened frozen blueberries
- ½ cup orange juice
- 1 teaspoon unflavored gelatin
- ¼ cup water
- ¼ teaspoon grated orange peel
- 2 tablespoons honey
- ¼ cup sugar
- ½ cup miniature marshmallows, halved
- 1 cup plain low-fat yogurt, stirred

IN A BLENDER OR FOOD PROCESSOR fitted with a metal blade, finely chop blueberries with orange juice; set aside. In small saucepan, sprinkle gelatin over water; let stand 1 minute. Cook and stir over low heat until gelatin dissolves. Remove from heat; add orange peel, honey, sugar, puréed berry mixture, marshmallows, and yogurt. Freeze in ice cream maker according to manufacturer's directions; or follow refrigerator-freezer instructions on page 11.

1 serving contains:

Cal	Carb	Fat	Chol	Calcium
130	29g	1g	2mg	81mg

Cranberry-Orange Sherbet

RATHER THAN A HEAVY DESSERT AT THE END OF A HOLIDAY MEAL, BEGIN A NEW TRADITION AND INTRODUCE GUESTS TO THIS LIGHT DISH.

Makes about 2 quarts

- 2 cups sugar
- 1 (.25-ounce) envelope unflavored gelatin
- 2 teaspoons grated orange peel
- 3 cups milk
- 2 cups fresh or frozen whole cranberries, thawed
- 1 cup orange juice

IN A MEDIUM SAUCEPAN, combine sugar, gelatin, and orange peel. Stir in milk. Stir over low heat until sugar and gelatin dissolve; set aside. In blender or food processor fitted with metal blade, purée cranberries and orange juice. Stir into milk mixture until blended. Pour into ice cream canister. Freeze in ice cream maker according to manufacturer's directions; or follow refrigerator-freezer instructions on page 11.

1 serving contains:

Cal	Carb	Fat	Chol	Calcium
179	41g	1g	5mg	79mg

Cranberry-Wine Sorbet

THE WONDERFUL AROMA OF CRANBERRIES COOKING IN WINE IS ALMOST AS GOOD AS EATING THE SORBET.

Makes about 1 quart

2	cups fresh or frozen whole cranberries, thawed
1/2	cup burgundy wine
1 1/2	cups orange juice
1	cup sugar
1	teaspoon grated orange peel

IN A MEDIUM SAUCEPAN, combine all ingredients. Stir over medium heat until cranberries are soft and break open. Pour into a fine strainer over a medium bowl. Press as much juice and pulp as possible through strainer with back of a spoon; discard remaining pulp. Cool strained purée to room temperature. Pour into ice cream canister. Freeze in ice cream maker according to manufacturer's directions; or follow refrigerator-freezer instructions on page 11.

1 serving contains:

Cal	Carb	Fat	Chol	Calcium
187	44g	0g	0g	10mg

Watermelon-Berry Sorbet

DISCOVER THE UNUSUAL COMBINATION THAT RASPBERRIES AND WATERMELON PRODUCE!

| Makes about 1 quart |

- **2** cups fresh or frozen raspberries, thawed
- **3** cups cubed watermelon, seeded
- **1** teaspoon unflavored gelatin
- **¼** cup water
- **12** (1-gram) packets Equal® sugar substitute

IN BLENDER OR FOOD PROCESSOR fitted with metal blade, purée raspberries. Strain and discard seeds. Set purée aside. Purée watermelon; set aside. In small saucepan, sprinkle gelatin over water; let stand 1 minute. Cook and stir over low heat until gelatin dissolves. Combine raspberry and melon purées, gelatin mixture, and sugar substitute. Pour into ice cream canister. Freeze in ice cream maker according to manufacturer's directions; or follow refrigerator-freezer instructions on page 11.

1 serving contains:

Cal	Carb	Fat	Chol	Calcium
53	10g	1g	0mg	16

Citrus Fruits

LEMON
Lemon Ice Cream
Lemon Cheesecake Ice Cream
Lemon-Tangerine Sorbet
Lemon-Ricotta Frozen Yogurt

LIME
Velvet Lime Ice Cream
Key Lime Frozen Yogurt

GRAPEFRUIT
Grapefruit-Mint Gelato

ORANGE
Grand Marnier Ice Cream
California Orange Sherbet

Orange Glow Frozen Yogurt
Avocado-Orange Cups
Orange-Cranberry-Nut Frozen
   Yogurt

TANGERINE
Tangerine Ice Cream
Tangerine-Chocolate Chip Ice
   Cream
Tangerine-Raspberry Sorbet
Sugar-Free Tangerine Frozen
   Yogurt
Tangerine-Pistachio Swirl Frozen
   Yogurt

Lemon Ice Cream

A FEW INGREDIENTS MAKE A REFRESHING DISH. YOU'LL NEVER FORGET THIS SPECIAL LEMON TREAT!

Makes about 1 quart

¼	cup lemon juice
1	cup sugar
½	teaspoon grated lemon peel
2	cups half-and-half

IN A MEDIUM BOWL, combine lemon juice and sugar; stir to blend. Stir in lemon peel and half-and-half. Pour into ice cream canister. Freeze in ice cream maker according to manufacturer's directions; or follow refrigerator-freezer instructions on page 11.

1 serving contains:

Cal	Carb	Fat	Chol	Calcium
236	38g	9g	30mg	86mg

Lemon-Ricotta Frozen Yogurt

ITALIAN CHEESE HELPS PRODUCE A FIRST COUSIN OF THE EVER-POPULAR LEMON CHEESECAKE.

Makes about 1 quart

- ¼ cup low-fat milk
- 1 teaspoon unflavored gelatin
- 1 cup ricotta cheese
- ¾ cup sugar
- ½ teaspoon grated lemon peel
- ¼ cup lemon juice
- 1½ cups plain low-fat yogurt, stirred

IN A SMALL SAUCEPAN, combine milk and gelatin; let stand 1 minute. Stir over low heat until gelatin dissolves. Remove from heat; set aside. In blender or food processor fitted with metal blade, combine ricotta cheese, sugar, and lemon peel. Process until ricotta is smooth. Stir in lemon juice, dissolved gelatin, and yogurt. Freeze in ice cream maker according to manufacturer's directions; or follow refrigerator-freezer instructions on page 11.

1 serving contains:

Cal	Carb	Fat	Chol	Calcium
216	32g	6g	25mg	211mg

Velvet Lime Ice Cream

MARSHMALLOWS AND CREAM HELP CREATE AN INCREDIBLY LIGHT AND SMOOTH ICE CREAM.

Makes about 1 quart

1	cup milk
¾	cup sugar
2	eggs, beaten
½	teaspoon grated lemon peel
1	cup miniature marshmallows
½	cup lime juice
1	cup whipping cream
4 or 5	drops green food coloring

IN A MEDIUM SAUCEPAN, combine milk, sugar, beaten eggs, and lemon peel. Cook and stir over low heat until mixture is thickened and coats a spoon; remove from heat. Stir in marshmallows until melted. Add lime juice, whipping cream, and food coloring until blended. Pour into ice cream canister. Freeze in ice cream maker according to manufacturer's directions; or follow refrigerator-freezer instructions on page 11.

1 serving contains:

Cal	Carb	Fat	Chol	Calcium
313	36g	18g	131mg	85mg

Key Lime Frozen Yogurt

JUST THREE INGREDIENTS. WHAT COULD BE MORE APPEALING AND TIMESAVING THAN THIS TANTALIZING SWEET-SOUR COMBINATION?

Makes about 1 quart

- 1 cup plain low-fat yogurt, stirred
- 1 (14-ounce) can sweetened condensed milk
- 1 (6-ounce) can frozen limeade concentrate, undiluted and partially thawed

IN A MEDIUM BOWL, combine yogurt and condensed milk. Stir in undiluted and partially thawed limeade concentrate. Freeze in ice cream maker according to manufacturer's directions; or follow refrigerator-freezer instructions on page 11.

1 serving contains:

Cal	Carb	Fat	Chol	Calcium
380	69g	8g	33mg	330mg

Grapefruit-Mint Gelato

SURPRISE GUESTS WITH THIS FANTASTIC FLAVOR. SERVE THIS ITALIAN ICE AFTER DINNER.

Makes about 1 quart

1	cup sugar
1	cup water
1	cup fresh mint leaves and stems
2	cups grapefruit juice
3 or 4	drops green food coloring

IN A MEDIUM SAUCEPAN, combine sugar, water, and mint. Stir over medium heat until mixture comes to a boil. Simmer over low heat 5 minutes; set aside. Cover and let stand about 10 minutes. Place a fine strainer over a large bowl. Pour syrup through strainer to remove mint; discard mint. Stir in grapefruit juice and food coloring. Pour into ice cream canister. Freeze in ice cream maker according to manufacturer's directions; or follow refrigerator-freezer instructions on page 11.

1 serving contains:

Cal	Carb	Fat	Chol	Calcium
161	41g	0g	0mg	9mg

Grand Marnier Ice Cream

AN ELEGANT FINISH, THE CROWNING GLORY, TO A GOURMET MEAL.

Makes about 1 quart

- ⅓ cup sugar
- ½ cup orange juice
- ¼ cup water
- ½ teaspoon grated orange peel
- 2 egg yolks, beaten
- 3 tablespoons Grand Marnier® liqueur
- 1½ cups half-and-half or whipping cream

IN A MEDIUM SAUCEPAN, combine sugar, orange juice, water, orange peel, and beaten egg yolks. Stir constantly over medium heat until mixture thickens. Cool slightly; stir in Grand Marnier and half-and-half or whipping cream. Pour into ice cream canister. Freeze in ice cream maker according to manufacturer's directions; or follow refrigerator-freezer instructions on page 11.

1 serving contains:

Cal	Carb	Fat	Chol	Calcium
162	19g	9g	93mg	74mg

California Orange Sherbet

WHEN YOU COMBINE ORANGE WITH A HINT OF LEMON, THE RESULTS TASTE GREAT.

Makes about 2 quarts

2	cups orange juice
2	tablespoons lemon juice
1⅓	cups sugar
3	cups milk
3 or 4	drops orange food coloring

IN A MEDIUM BOWL, combine orange juice, lemon juice, and sugar. Stir until sugar dissolves. Stir in milk and food coloring until blended. Pour into ice cream canister. Freeze in ice cream maker according to manufacturer's directions; or follow refrigerator-freezer instructions on page 11.

1 serving contains:

Cal	Carb	Fat	Chol	Calcium
143	30g	2g	8mg	77mg

Orange Glow Frozen Yogurt

SPARKLING ORANGE FLAVOR MAKES A FRESH FINALE TO A SPECIAL DINNER.

Makes about 1 quart

1	orange
2/3	cup sugar
1	teaspoon unflavored gelatin
1 1/2	cups orange juice
2	tablespoons honey
1 1/2	cups plain low-fat yogurt, stirred

WITH ZESTER OR PARING KNIFE, cut peel from orange, being careful not to include any of the bitter white part. Combine peel with sugar in blender or food processor fitted with metal blade; process until finely minced. Set aside. In a medium saucepan, combine gelatin and orange juice; let stand one minute. Stir over low heat until gelatin dissolves. Add honey. Combine with processed orange peel. Strain; discard peel. Cool. Stir in yogurt. Freeze in ice cream maker according to manufacturer's directions; or follow refrigerator-freezer instructions on page 11.

1 serving contains:

Cal	Carb	Fat	Chol	Calcium
186	42g	1g	4mg	127mg

Avocado-Orange Cups

AN EXCELLENT LUNCHEON DESSERT FOR AVOCADO LOVERS.

Makes 6 servings

3 large oranges

1 (.25-ounce) envelope
   unflavored gelatin

2 large ripe avocados, peeled

½ cup sugar

1 cup dairy sour cream

Whipped cream, if desired

CUT ORANGES in half crosswise. Scoop pulp from orange halves without damaging shells; reserve shells. Spoon pulp into strainer over a small saucepan. Press juice from pulp into pan; discard pulp or use for another purpose. Reserve ½ cup orange juice in saucepan; use remaining juice for another purpose. Sprinkle gelatin over reserved orange juice to soften. Stir over very low heat until gelatin dissolves; set aside. Notch edges of reserved orange shells if desired; set aside. Pour gelatin mixture into blender or food processor. Cut avocados into pieces; puree with gelatin mixture. Add sugar; process 3 to 5 seconds to blend. In a small bowl, stir sour cream until smooth. Stir in avocado mixture. Spoon into reserved orange shells. Top with whipped cream, if desired. Cover with foil or plastic wrap. Place in freezer; freeze until firm, 3 to 6 hours.

1 serving contains:

Cal	Carb	Fat	Chol	Calcium
260	33g	14g	13mg	1mg

Orange-Cranberry-Nut Frozen Yogurt

FOR A CHANGE, SERVE THIS BEAUTIFUL DESSERT TO ENHANCE HOLIDAY ENTERTAINING.

Makes about 1 quart

- 1 large orange, peeled, seeded and cut into chunks
- 1 cup fresh cranberries
- ¾ cup sugar
- 2 tablespoons light corn syrup
- 1 teaspoon unflavored gelatin
- ¾ cup low-fat milk
- 1 cup plain low-fat yogurt, stirred
- ¼ cup finely chopped toasted pecans or walnuts

IN A BLENDER OR FOOD PROCESSOR fitted with metal blade, finely chop orange. Add cranberries, sugar, and corn syrup. Process until cranberries are finely chopped. In small saucepan, combine gelatin and milk; let stand about 1 minute. Stir over low heat until gelatin dissolves. Combine with cranberry mixture. Stir in yogurt and nuts. Freeze in ice cream maker according to manufacturer's directions; or follow refrigerator-freezer instructions on page 11.

1 serving contains:

Cal	Carb	Fat	Chol	Calcium
215	41g	5g	5mg	128mg

Tangerine Ice Cream

TANGERINES DELIVER INTENSE YET PLEASING FLAVOR.

Makes about 1½ quarts

- 1 cup sugar
- 1 (.25-ounce) envelope unflavored gelatin
- 2 cups milk
- 1 or 2 teaspoons grated tangerine peel
- 2 cups tangerine juice
- 1 cup half-and-half
- 3 or 4 drops orange food coloring, if desired

IN A LARGE BOWL, combine sugar and gelatin; set aside. In a small saucepan, heat milk almost to boiling. Stir into gelatin mixture until gelatin and sugar dissolve. Stir in tangerine peel and tangerine juice. Add half-and-half and food coloring, if desired. Pour into ice cream canister. Freeze in ice cream maker according to manufacturer's directions; or follow refrigerator-freezer instructions on page 11.

1 serving contains:

Cal	Carb	Fat	Chol	Calcium
163	28g	5g	16mg	93mg

Tangerine-Chocolate Chip Ice Cream

CHOCOLATE WITH TANGERINE IS A WINNING COMBINATION.

Makes about 1 quart

- ½ cup sugar
- 1½ teaspoons cornstarch
- 1 cup half-and-half
- ¼ cup light corn syrup
- 2 eggs, beaten
- 1½ cups tangerine juice
- 1 teaspoon grated tangerine peel
- 4 drops almond extract
- 1 (1-ounce) square semisweet chocolate

IN MEDIUM SAUCEPAN, combine sugar and cornstarch. Stir in half-and-half and corn syrup. Cook and stir over moderate heat until bubbly. Remove from heat. Slowly stir into beaten eggs. Return mixture to pan; cook and stir over low heat for 2 minutes. Stir in tangerine juice, peel, and almond extract; chill. Melt chocolate over hot water or in microwave. Slowly stir melted chocolate into chilled tangerine mixture. Pour into ice cream canister. Freeze in ice cream maker according to manufacturer's directions; or follow refrigerator-freezer instructions on page 11.

1 serving contains:

Cal	Carb	Fat	Chol	Calcium
232	38g	8g	86mg	65mg

Tangerine-Raspberry Sorbet

FOR A STRONGER TANGERINE FLAVOR, USE MORE GRATED PEEL.

Makes about 1 quart

5	medium tangerines
1 or 2	teaspoons grated tangerine peel
1½	cups fresh or frozen raspberries, thawed
½	cup light corn syrup
¼	cup dry white wine

PEEL TANGERINES and remove seeds. Purée tangerine sections, raspberries, and grated tangerine peel in blender or food processor fitted with a metal blade. Place a fine strainer over a medium bowl. Pour puréed mixture into strainer; lightly press with back of a spoon to remove pulp and seeds. Discard pulp and seeds. Stir in corn syrup and wine. Pour into ice cream canister. Freeze in ice cream maker according to manufacturer's directions; or follow refrigerator-freezer instructions on page 11.

1 serving contains:

Cal	Carb	Fat	Chol	Calcium
130	33g	0g	0mg	19mg

Sugar-Free Tangerine Frozen Yogurt

NO ONE WILL BELIEVE YOU MADE THIS DELICIOUS FROZEN YOGURT WITHOUT SUGAR.

Makes about 1 quart

- ¼ cup water and 1 teaspoon unflavored gelatin
- ½ teaspoon grated tangerine peel
- 1 cup tangerine juice (6 to 8 small tangerines)
- 12 (1-gram) packets Equal® sugar substitute
- 1 cup plain fat-free yogurt, stirred
- 1 egg white
- ⅓ cup water
- ⅓ cup fat-free dry milk

IN A SMALL SAUCEPAN, combine water and gelatin; let stand 1 minute. Stir over low heat until gelatin dissolves. In medium bowl, combine dissolved gelatin, tangerine peel, juice, and sugar substitute. Stir in yogurt. Beat egg white with ⅓ cup water and dry milk until stiff but not dry. Fold into tangerine yogurt mixture. Freeze in ice cream maker according to manufacturer's directions; or follow refrigerator-freezer instructions on page 11.

1 serving contains:

Cal	Carb	Fat	Chol	Calcium
60	9g	0g	1mg`	109mg

Tangerine-Pistachio Swirl Frozen Yogurt

NATURAL PISTACHIOS, NOT THE KIND THAT HAVE BEEN DYED RED, BLEND BEST WITH THE GREEN FOOD COLORING IN THIS PISTACHIO SWIRL.

Makes about 1 quart

- ¾ cup low-fat milk
- ⅔ cup miniature or cut-up large marshmallows
- ½ cup pistachios
- 4 or 5 drops green food coloring, optional
- 1 teaspoon unflavored gelatin

- ½ cup low-fat milk
- 1½ cups tangerine juice
- ¾ cup sugar
- ½ teaspoon vanilla extract
- 1 cup plain low-fat yogurt, stirred

IN A SMALL SAUCEPAN, combine ¾ cup milk and marshmallows. Cook and stir over low heat until marshmallows dissolve. Remove from heat; pour into blender or food processor fitted with a metal blade. Add nuts and process until almost smooth. While processing, add food coloring (if desired) 1 drop at a time. Refrigerate. In small saucepan, sprinkle gelatin over ½ cup milk; let stand 1 minute. Then cook and stir over low heat just until gelatin dissolves. Remove from heat; cool. In medium bowl, combine cooled gelatin mixture, tangerine juice, sugar, vanilla, and yogurt. Stir until sugar is dissolved. Freeze in ice cream maker according to manufacturer's directions. When frozen, stir in pistachio-marshmallow mixture just enough to create a swirled effect. Or follow refrigerator-freezer instructions on page 11, and stir in pistachio-marshmallow mixture after final processing or beating.

1 serving contains:

Cal	Carb	Fat	Chol	Calcium
257	44g	7g	6mg	175mg

Orchard Fruits

APPLE
Spicy Applesauce Ice Cream
Apple Calvados Ice Cream
Sparkling Apple Sorbet
Apple-Maple Frozen Yogurt
Cinnamon-Apple Frozen Yogurt

APRICOT
Apricot-Ginger Ice Cream
Fresh Apricot Frozen Yogurt
Apricot-Honey Frozen Yogurt

CHERRY
Cherry-Berry Ice Cream
Cherry-Cranberry Sorbet
Bing Cherry-Cranberry Frozen
    Yogurt

NECTARINE
Nectarine Ice Cream
Nectarine Sorbet
Toasted Almond-Nectarine Frozen
    Yogurt

PEACH
Favorite Peach Ice Cream
Ginger-Peach Ice Cream

Peach Custard Ice Cream
Peachy Almond Frozen Yogurt
Maple-Peach Frozen Yogurt
Peach-Macaroon Frozen Yogurt
Peach-Strawberry Frozen Yogurt

PEAR
Pear-Mint Sorbet
Ginger-Pear Ice Cream
Pear-and-Port Frozen Yogurt

PLUM
Fresh Plum Ice Cream
Plum-Grape Sherbet
Plum-Orange Sorbet
Spicy Plum Frozen Yogurt

POMEGRANATE
Pomegranate Granita
Fresh Pomegranate Frozen Yogurt

PERSIMMON
Persimmon Frozen Yogurt

Spicy Applesauce Ice Cream

DELICATE APPLE FLAVOR LACED WITH YOUR FAVORITE SPICES. GREAT WITH APPLE PIE!

Makes about 2 quarts

1	(.25-ounce) envelope unflavored gelatin
1	(14-ounce) jar unsweetened applesauce
¾	cup lightly packed brown sugar
2	eggs, beaten
½	teaspoon ground cinnamon
¼	teaspoon ground mace
⅛	teaspoon ground ginger
1	cup dairy sour cream
2	cups half-and-half

IN A MEDIUM SAUCEPAN, sprinkle gelatin over applesauce. Stir to blend; let stand one minute. Stir in brown sugar, beaten eggs, cinnamon, mace, and ginger. Cook and stir over low heat until gelatin dissolves and mixture thickens slightly. Cool to lukewarm. Stir in sour cream and half-and-half. Pour into ice cream canister. Freeze in ice cream maker according to manufacturer's directions; or follow refrigerator-freezer instructions on page 11.

1 serving contains:

Cal	Carb	Fat	Chol	Calcium
174	20g	10g	59mg	83mg

Apple Calvados Ice Cream

CALVADOS IS AN APPLE BRANDY THAT CONTRIBUTES AN INTERESTING EUROPEAN ACCENT.

Makes about 1 quart

1	teaspoon unflavored gelatin
1	cup low-fat milk
1	large apple, peeled, cored, quartered
¼	cup Calvados (apple brandy)
⅓	cup sugar
2	tablespoons light corn syrup
1	cup whipping cream

IN A SMALL SAUCEPAN, sprinkle gelatin over milk; let stand 1 minute. Stir over low heat until gelatin dissolves. Remove from heat; cool. In blender or food processor fitted with a metal blade, combine apple, Calvados, sugar, and corn syrup. Process until apple is finely chopped. Combine with gelatin-milk mixture and whipping cream. Pour into ice cream canister. Freeze in ice cream maker according to manufacturer's directions; or follow refrigerator-freezer instructions on page 11.

1 serving contains:

Cal	Carb	Fat	Chol	Calcium
261	15g	25g	56mg	79mg

Sparkling Apple Sorbet

SPARKLING APPLE JUICE PROVIDES A REFRESHING TWIST TO THIS SORBET.

Makes about 1 quart

⅓	cup sugar
⅓	cup light corn syrup
⅓	cup water
3	tart apples, peeled, cored, quartered
2	teaspoons lemon juice
1½	cups sparkling apple juice
⅛	teaspoon ground nutmeg

IN A SMALL SAUCEPAN, combine sugar, corn syrup, and water. Stir over medium heat until sugar dissolves; cool. In blender or food processor fitted with a metal blade, combine cooled sugar, syrup, apples, and lemon juice; process until apples are finely chopped. Combine apple mixture, apple juice, and nutmeg. Pour into ice cream canister. Freeze in ice cream maker according to manufacturer's directions; or follow refrigerator-freezer instructions on page 11.

1 serving contains:

Cal	Carb	Fat	Chol	Calcium
163	43g	0g	0mg	5mg

Apple-Maple Frozen Yogurt

MAPLE SYRUP WITH APPLE IS REMINISCENT OF FAVORITE FOODS FROM OUR CHILDHOOD DAYS.

Makes about 1 quart

- 1 cooking apple, peeled, cored, and finely chopped
- 1 cup maple syrup
- ⅛ teaspoon ground cardamom
- 2 teaspoons unflavored gelatin
- ½ cup low-fat milk
- 1 cup plain low-fat yogurt, stirred

IN A MEDIUM SAUCEPAN, combine apple, maple syrup, and cardamom. Cover and simmer until apple pieces are very soft. In the meantime, sprinkle gelatin over milk; let stand 1 minute. Add to hot apple mixture. Stir until gelatin is dissolved. Cool; add yogurt. Freeze in ice cream maker according to manufacturer's directions; or follow refrigerator-freezer instructions on page 11.

1 serving contains:

Cal	Carb	Fat	Chol	Calcium
189	43g	1g	3mg	137mg

Cinnamon-Apple Frozen Yogurt

A WELCOME TASTE SENSATION, BOTH SPICY-HOT AND COLD IN THE SAME SPOONFUL. TO SHORTEN THE PREPARATION TIME ON THIS POPULAR FLAVOR COMBINATION, SUBSTITUTE 1 CUP UNSWEETENED APPLESAUCE FOR THE 2 TART APPLES AND LEMON JUICE.

Makes about 1 quart

2	small tart apples, peeled, cored and cut into wedges
1½	teaspoons lemon juice
½	cup sugar
1	teaspoon cornstarch
1	cup low-fat milk
½	cup red-hot cinnamon candies
1	cup plain low-fat yogurt, stirred

IN A BLENDER OR FOOD PROCESSOR fitted with a metal blade, combine apple wedges and lemon juice. Process until puréed; set aside. In medium saucepan, combine sugar and cornstarch. Stir in milk and cinnamon candies. Cook and stir over medium-low heat until mixture simmers. Cook and stir 1 minute longer or until cinnamon candies are dissolved. Remove from heat; stir in puréed apples. Cool; stir in yogurt. Freeze in ice cream maker according to manufacturer's directions; or follow refrigerator-freezer instructions on page 11.

1 serving contains:

Cal	Carb	Fat	Chol	Calcium
165	36g	1g	4mg	127mg

Apricot-Ginger Ice Cream

FRESH GINGER ADDS A SPICY WARMTH TO THIS PLEASING APRICOT DESSERT.

Makes about 1 quart

- 2 tablespoons water
- 1 teaspoon unflavored gelatin
- ¾ cup dried apricots (about 3 ounces)
- ¾ cup orange juice
- 2 teaspoons grated fresh ginger
- 3 (1-gram) packets Sweet 'N Low® sugar substitue
- ¼ cup sugar
- 1½ cups half-and-half
- ⅛ teaspoon almond extract

COMBINE WATER AND GELATIN; let stand at least 1 minute. In small saucepan, combine apricots, orange juice, and ginger. Simmer, covered, over low heat about 8 minutes or until apricots are soft. Remove from heat; immediately stir in softened gelatin. In blender or food processor fitted with a metal blade, combine cooked mixture, sugar substitute, and sugar. Process until puréed. Cool. Add half-and-half and almond extract. Pour into ice cream canister. Freeze in ice cream maker according to manufacturer's directions; or follow refrigerator-freezer instructions on page 11.

1 serving contains:

Cal	Carb	Fat	Chol	Calcium
87	22g	0g	0mg	11mg

Fresh Apricot Frozen Yogurt

ENJOY THE SHORT SEASON FOR FRESH APRICOTS; ONLY USE FULLY RIPE ONES FOR BEST FLAVOR.

Makes about 1 quart

3 large ripe fresh apricots, pitted and coarsely chopped (about 10 ounces)

$\frac{1}{2}$ cup sugar

$\frac{1}{4}$ cup light corn syrup

1 tablespoon lemon juice

$\frac{1}{8}$ teaspoon almond extract

$\frac{3}{4}$ cup low-fat milk

1 cup plain low-fat yogurt, stirred

IN A BLENDER OR FOOD PROCESSOR fitted with a metal blade, combine apricots, sugar, corn syrup, lemon juice, and almond extract. Process until finely chopped. Stir in milk and yogurt. Freeze in ice cream maker according to manufacturer's directions; or follow refrigerator-freezer instructions on page 11.

1 serving contains:

Cal	Carb	Fat	Chol	Calcium
151	34g	1g	4mg	115mg

Apricot-Honey Frozen Yogurt

CANNED APRICOTS ARE ACCENTED WITH A HINT OF AMARETTO LIQUEUR. WE KEEP A CAN OF APRICOTS ON HAND SO THIS FROZEN TREAT CAN BE MADE ANY DAY OF THE YEAR.

Makes about 1 quart

1	(16- or 17-ounce) can unpeeled apricot halves in heavy syrup
⅓	cup sugar
2	teaspoons cornstarch
2	tablespoons honey
1½	cups plain low-fat yogurt, stirred
1	tablespoon Amaretto® almond-flavored liqueur

IN A BLENDER OR FOOD PROCESSOR fitted with a metal blade, purée apricots and their syrup; set aside. In medium saucepan, combine sugar and coarnstarch. Stir in honey and purée apricots. Cook and stir over medium heat until slightly thickened. Remove from heat; cool to lukewarm. Add yogurt and Amaretto liqueur. Freeze in ice cream maker according to manufacturer's directions; or follow refrigerator-freezer instructions on page 11.

1 serving contains:

Cal	Carb	Fat	Chol	Calcium
178	39g	1g	4mg	119mg

Cherry-Berry Ice Cream

BEAUTIFUL COLOR AND AN EXPLOSION OF FLAVOR.

Makes about 1 quart

2 cups fresh or frozen dark sweet cherries, pitted, thawed

1 cup fresh or frozen blackberries or boysenberries, thawed

1 teaspoon unflavored gelatin

2 tablespoons water

1 cup half-and-half

½ cup sugar

2 tablespoons light corn syrup

IN A BLENDER OR FOOD PROCESSOR fitted with a metal blade, purée cherries; pour into medium bowl. Purée berries; strain to remove seeds. Add strained berries to cherries. Sprinkle gelatin over water; let stand 1 minute. Stir over low heat until gelatin dissolves. Combine fruit purée, dissolved gelatin, half-and-half, sugar, and corn syrup. Stir until sugar dissolves. Pour into ice cream canister. Freeze in ice cream maker according to manufacturer's directions; or follow refrigerator-freezer instructions on page 11.

1 serving contains:

Cal	Carb	Fat	Chol	Calcium
185	35g	5g	15mg	58mg

Cherry-Cranberry Sorbet

ALTHOUGH WE PREFER TO USE FRESH FRUIT, IT ISN'T ALWAYS AVAILABLE, SO IF NEED BE, SUBSTITUTE WITH 2 (16-OUNCE) CANS OF DRAINED, PITTED SWEET CHERRIES; REDUCE SUGAR TO ½ CUP.

Makes about 2 quarts

- 4 cups fresh, ripe, sweet dark cherries, pitted
- ⅔ cup sugar
- ½ cup light corn syrup
- 2 cups cranberry juice

IN A BLENDER OR FOOD PROCESSOR fitted with a metal blade, purée cherries, sugar, and corn syrup. Add cranberry juice; process 3 to 5 seconds. Pour into ice cream canister. Freeze in ice cream maker according to manufacturer's directions; or follow refrigerator-freezer instructions on page 11.

1 serving contains:

Cal	Carb	Fat	Chol	Calcium
140	36g	1g	0mg	9mg

Bing Cherry-Cranberry Frozen Yogurt

SWEET DARK CHERRIES BLEND BEAUTIFULLY WITH CRANBERRY JUICE; DON'T USE THE BRIGHT-RED PIE CHERRIES AS THEY ARE TOO TART.

Makes about 1 quart

1   cup cranberry juice cocktail

1   teaspoon unflavored gelatin

1   cup fresh or frozen, pitted Bing sweet cherries

2/3 cup sugar

1   cup plain low-fat yogurt, stirred

IN A SMALL PAN, combine cranberry juice and gelatin; let stand 1 minute. Cook and stir over low heat until gelatin dissolves. In a blender or food processor fitted with a metal blade, combine pitted cherries and sugar; process until almost smooth. Combine with dissolved gelatin. Stir in yogurt. Freeze in ice cream maker according to manufacturer's directions; or follow refrigerator-freezer instructions on page 11.

1 serving contains:

Cal	Carb	Fat	Chol	Calcium
155	35g	1g	2mg	80mg

Nectarine Ice Cream

**ALMOND FLAVORING ACCENTUATES THE FLAVOR OF FRESH NECTARINES.
YOU CAN SUBSTITUTE FRESH OR FROZEN PEACHES FOR NECTARINES.**

Makes about 1 quart

1	egg, beaten
½	cup sugar
½	cup low-fat milk
2	tablespoons light corn syrup
3	ripe nectarines, peeled, pitted, quartered
½	teaspoon vanilla extract
⅛	teaspoon almond extract
½	cup whipping cream

IN A SMALL SAUCEPAN, combine beaten egg, sugar, milk, and corn syrup. Cook and stir over low heat until thickened; cool. Purée nectarines in blender or food processor fitted with a metal blade. Combine cooled egg-milk mixture, puréed nectarines, vanilla and almond extract, and whipping cream. Pour into ice cream canister. Freeze in ice cream maker according to manufacturer's directions; or follow refrigerator-freezer instructions on page 11.

1 serving contains:

Cal	Carb	Fat	Chol	Calcium
208	32g	9g	63mg	46mg

Nectarine Sorbet

SAVOR THAT SPECIAL FRESH TASTE OF RIPE FRUIT.

Makes about 2 quarts

$2/3$	cup sugar
$2/3$	cup light corn syrup
1	cup water
1	teaspoon grated lemon peel
2	tablespoons lemon juice
8 or 9	large ripe nectarines, peeled, pitted, quartered

IN A SMALL SAUCEPAN, combine sugar, corn syrup, water, and lemon peel. Stir over medium heat until mixture comes to a boil. Stir in lemon juice. Cool to room temperature. In blender or food processor fitted with a metal blade, purée nectarines. Add syrup mixture; process 2 to 3 seconds to blend. Pour into ice cream canister. Freeze in ice cream maker according to manufacturer's directions; or follow refrigerator-freezer instructions on page 11.

1 serving contains:

Cal	Carb	Fat	Chol	Calcium
140	36g	0g	0mg	6mg

Toasted Almond-Nectarine Frozen Yogurt

TOASTED ALMONDS JOIN FORCES WITH NECTARINES TO ENHANCE BOTH TASTE AND TEXTURE.

Makes about 1 quart

- ¼ cup toasted slivered almonds
- ½ cup sugar
- ¼ teaspoon ground nutmeg
- ¼ cup low-fat milk
- 1 teaspoon unflavored gelatin
- 4 medium ripe nectarines, pitted and quartered
- ¼ cup light corn syrup
- 1 cup plain low-fat yogurt, stirred

IN A BLENDER OR FOOD PROCESSOR fitted with a metal blade, combine toasted almonds, sugar, and nutmeg. Process until nuts are finely chopped; set aside in medium bowl. In small saucepan, combine milk and gelatin; let stand 1 minute. Cook and stir over low heat until gelatin dissolves; set aside. Purée nectarines and corn syrup in blender or food processor; combine with almond mixture and dissolved gelatin. Stir in yogurt. Freeze in ice cream maker according to manufacturer's directions; or follow refrigerator-freezer instructions on page 11.

1 serving contains:

Cal	Carb	Fat	Chol	Calcium
206	42g	4g	3mg	105mg

Favorite Peach Ice Cream

**SAVOR FRESH PEACHES AT THEIR FLAVOR PEAK. IT'S HARD TO BELIEVE
THIS RICH, SMOOTH ICE CREAM IS MADE WITHOUT EGGS.**

Makes about 1 quart

- 2 teaspoons cornstarch
- ½ cup sugar
- 1 (12-ounce) can low-fat evaporated milk
- 2 tablespoons light corn syrup
- 3 medium ripe peaches, peeled, pitted, quartered
- ½ cup half-and-half

IN A MEDIUM SAUCEPAN, combine cornstarch and sugar. Stir in evaporated milk and corn syrup. Cook and stir over medium heat until bubbly; cook 1 minute longer. Set aside to cool. In blender or food processor fitted with a metal blade, finely chop peaches. Combine chopped peaches, cooled milk mixture, and half-and-half. Pour into ice cream canister. Freeze in ice cream maker according to manufacturer's directions; or follow refrigerator-freezer instructions on page 11.

1 serving contains:

Cal	Carb	Fat	Chol	Calcium
202	39g	4g	13mg	203mg

Ginger-Peach Ice Cream

CHOPPED CHINESE ALMOND COOKIES PROVIDE AN UNUSUAL CONTRAST IN TASTE AND TEXTURE.

Makes about 1 quart

- 1   teaspoon unflavored gelatin
- 1   cup half-and-half
- 1   tablespoon chopped crystallized ginger
- ⅓   cup sugar
- 2   tablespoons light corn syrup
- 3   ripe peaches, peeled, pitted, sliced
- 6   Chinese almond cookies, coarsely chopped (about 1 cup)

IN A SMALL SAUCEPAN, sprinkle gelatin over half-and-half; let stand 1 minute. Cook and stir over low heat until gelatin dissolves. Add ginger, sugar, and corn syrup. In blender or food processor fitted with a metal blade, finely chop peaches. Combine ginger mixture with chopped peaches. Add half of chopped cookies; reserve remaining half. Pour into ice cream canister. Freeze in ice cream maker according to manufacturer's directions. When frozen, stir in reserved chopped cookies before serving; or follow refrigerator-freezer instructions on page 11 and stir in reserved chopped cookies after final processing or beating.

1 serving contains:

Cal	Carb	Fat	Chol	Calcium
494	111g	8g	19mg	67mg

Peach Custard Ice Cream

INDULGE YOURSELF WITH THIS VELVETY-SMOOTH DESSERT. IT HAS UNBEATABLE PEACH FLAVOR.

Makes about 2 quarts

3	eggs
1	cup sugar
1	cup milk
$\frac{1}{8}$	teaspoon almond extract
$\frac{1}{2}$	teaspoon vanilla extract
2	cups half-and-half
4	large fresh peaches, peeled, pitted, sliced

IN A MEDIUM BOWL, beat eggs until thick and lemon-colored, about 5 minutes. Gradually beat in sugar; set aside. In a medium saucepan, combine beaten egg mixture and milk. Cook and stir over low heat until slightly thickened and mixture coats a spoon. Stir in almond extract, vanilla extract, and half-and-half. Cool to room temperature. Purée peaches in blender or food processor fitted with a metal blade. Stir into custard mixture. Pour into ice cream canister. Freeze in ice cream maker according to manufacturer's directions; or follow refrigerator-freezer instructions on page 11.

1 serving contains:

Cal	Carb	Fat	Chol	Calcium
171	25g	7g	71mg	75mg

Peachy Almond Frozen Yogurt

SWEETENED ALMOND PASTE CONTRIBUTES JUST THE RIGHT ACCENT TO FRESH PEACHES.

Makes about 1 quart

- 3 medium ripe peaches, peeled and sliced
- 2 tablespoons almond paste
- ½ cup sugar
- ¾ cup evaporated low-fat milk
- 1 cup plain low-fat yogurt, stirred

IN A BLENDER OR FOOD PROCESSOR fitted with a metal blade, combine peaches, almond paste, and sugar. Process until peaches are finely chopped. Stir in milk and yogurt. Freeze in ice cream maker according to manufacturer's directions; or follow refrigerator-freezer instructions on page 11.

1 serving contains:

Cal	Carb	Fat	Chol	Calcium
162	31g	3g	5mg	175mg

Maple-Peach Frozen Yogurt

FANS OF MAPLE SYRUP IN PARTICULAR WILL LOVE THIS FLAVOR COMBINATION.

Makes about 1 quart

3	large ripe peaches, peeled and chopped
¼	cup sugar
1	teaspoon unflavored gelatin
½	cup low-fat milk
⅓	cup maple-flavored syrup
1	cup plain low-fat yogurt, stirred

IN A BLENDER OR FOOD PROCESSOR fitted with a metal blade, combine peaches and sugar. Process until peaches are finely chopped but not puréed. Pour into medium bowl. In small saucepan, sprinkle gelatin over milk; let stand 1 minute. Cook and stir over low heat until gelatin dissolves. Add to chopped peach mixture; then stir in maple syrup and yogurt. Freeze in ice cream maker according to manufacturer's directions; or follow refrigerator-freezer instructions on page 11.

1 serving contains:

Cal	Carb	Fat	Chol	Calcium
148	33g	1g	3mg	116mg

Peach-Macaroon Frozen Yogurt

ITALIAN MACAROONS CAN BE PURCHASED YEAR-ROUND. THEY COME PACKAGED IN TINS THAT GUARANTEE FRESHNESS FOR MONTHS. MACAROONS ENHANCE THE TASTE OF THIS YOGURT, AND PROVIDE A WELCOME CRUNCH TOO.

Makes about 1 quart

- ½ cup low-fat milk
- 1 teaspoon unflavored gelatin
- ½ cup sugar
- ⅛ cup light corn syrup
- ⅛ teaspoon ground nutmeg
- 4 medium ripe peaches, peeled and sliced
- ¾ cup plain low-fat yogurt, stirred
- 4 (2-inch-diameter) crisp macaroon cookies, coarsely crumbled

IN A SMALL SAUCEPAN, combine milk and gelatin; let stand 1 minute. Cook and stir over low heat until gelatin dissolves. Remove from heat. Stir in sugar, corn syrup, and nutmeg; set aside. In blender or food processor fitted with a metal blade, finely chop peaches. In medium bowl, combine peaches and gelatin mixture; stir in yogurt. Freeze in ice cream maker according to manufacturer's directions. When frozen, fold in crumbled macaroons. Or follow refrigerator-freezer instructions on page 11.

1 serving contains:

Cal	Carb	Fat	Chol	Calcium
206	44g	3g	3mg	86mg

Peach-Strawberry Frozen Yogurt

SERVE OVER FRESH PEACHES AND GARNISH WITH A SPRINKLE OF BERRIES.

Makes about 1 quart

- 1 cup fresh or frozen unsweetened strawberries
- 2 medium ripe peaches, peeled and sliced
- 1 teaspoon lemon juice
- ¾ cup plain low-fat yogurt, stirred
- 1 (14-ounce) can sweetened condensed milk

IN A BLENDER OR FOOD PROCESSOR fitted with a metal blade, combine strawberries, peaches, and lemon juice. Process until fruit is finely chopped. In a medium bowl, combine yogurt and condensed milk. Gradually stir in fruit mixture. Freeze in ice cream maker according to manufacturer's directions; or follow refrigerator-freezer instructions on page 11.

1 serving contains:

Cal	Carb	Fat	Chol	Calcium
328	56g	8g	32mg	315mg

Pear-Mint Sorbet

DUE TO WORLDWIDE SHIPMENT, WE NOW CAN ENJOY PEARS FOR MUCH OF THE YEAR. YOU'LL MAKE THE MOST OF THE PEARS' SWEET FLAVOR WITH THIS RECIPE.

Makes about 1 quart

- ⅓ cup sugar
- ⅓ cup water
- ¼ teaspoon grated lime peel
- 5 ripe pears, peeled, cored
- 1 tablespoon lime juice
- 3 tablespoons green crème de menthe liqueur

IN A SMALL SAUCEPAN, combine sugar, water, and lime peel. Stir over medium heat until mixture comes to a boil; set aside to cool. In blender or food processor fitted with a metal blade, purée pears and lime juice. Stir into cooled sugar mixture. Add crème de menthe. Pour into ice cream canister. Freeze in ice cream maker according to manufacturer's directions; or follow refrigerator-freezer instructions on page 11.

1 serving contains:

Cal	Carb	Fat	Chol	Calcium
157	36g	1g	0mg	16mg

Ginger-Pear Ice Cream

IF YOU WELCOME STRONGER GINGER FLAVOR, USE MORE GINGER; SOME PEOPLE PREFER JUST A HINT OF IT.

Makes about 2 quarts

4	fresh ripe pears, peeled, cored
2	tablespoons lemon juice
3 to 4	tablespoons chopped crystallized ginger
1	cup sugar
2	cups milk
1	cup whipping cream

IN A BLENDER OR FOOD PROCESSOR fitted with a metal blade, purée pears, lemon juice, and ginger. Pour into a large bowl. Stir in sugar until dissolved. Stir in milk and whipping cream. Pour into ice cream canister. Freeze in ice cream maker according to manufacturer's directions; or follow refrigerator-freezer instructions on page 11.

1 serving contains:

Cal	Carb	Fat	Chol	Calcium
215	34g	9g	33mg	84mg

Pear-and-Port Frozen Yogurt

PORT WINE AND FRESH PEARS MAKE PALATE-PLEASING COMPANIONS.

Makes about 1 quart

- 3 ripe pears, peeled, cored and cubed
- ½ cup port wine
- ¼ teaspoon grated lemon peel
- 1 stick cinnamon
- ½ cup sugar
- 2 teaspoons cornstarch
- ¼ cup low-fat milk
- 1 cup plain low-fat yogurt, stirred

IN A MEDIUM SAUCEPAN, combine pears, wine, lemon peel, cinnamon, and sugar. Cover and simmer about 3 minutes or until pears are almost soft; remove from heat. Dissolve cornstarch in milk. Stir into hot pear mixture. Return to heat and simmer another 3 or 4 minutes or until pears are soft. Discard cinnamon stick. Pour mixture into blender or food processor fitted with a metal blade. Process until finely chopped; cool. Stir in yogurt. Freeze in ice cream maker according to manufacturer's directions; or follow refrigerator-freezer instructions on page 11.

1 serving contains:

Cal	Carb	Fat	Chol	Calcium
177	36g	1g	3mg	98mg

Fresh Plum Ice Cream

WE PREFER THE BLACK PLUMS FOR THIS TREAT.

Makes about 1 quart

- 1 (8-ounce) carton Egg Beaters® egg substitute
- 1 cup low-fat milk
- ½ cup half-and-half
- ⅔ cup sugar
- 1 teaspoon lemon juice
- 4 ripe plums, pitted, quartered

IN A MEDIUM SAUCEPAN, combine egg substitute, milk, half-and-half, and sugar. Cook and stir over medium heat until very thick; cool. In blender or food processor fitted with a metal blade, purée lemon juice and plums. Place a fine strainer over a small bowl. Pour purée through strainer to remove peel, if desired. Stir into milk mixture. Pour into ice cream canister. Freeze in ice cream maker according to manufacturer's directions; or follow refrigerator-freezer instructions on page 11.

1 serving contains:

Cal	Carb	Fat	Chol	Calcium
189	31g	4g	9mg	95mg

Plum-Grape Sherbet

A REFRESHING TREAT FOR DESSERT OR A COOL SUMMER SNACK.

| Makes about 1 quart |

- 4 ripe plums, pitted, quartered
- 1 cup white grape juice
- ⅓ cup sugar
- 2 tablespoons light corn syrup
- 1 teaspoon unflavored gelatin
- 2 tablespoons water
- ½ cup whipping cream

IN A BLENDER OR FOOD PROCESSOR fitted with a metal blade, purée plums with grape juice, sugar, and corn syrup. Place a fine strainer over a small bowl. Pour purée through strainer to remove peel, if desired. Sprinkle gelatin over water; let stand 1 minute. Stir over low heat until gelatin dissolves. Combine plum purée, dissolved gelatin and whipping cream. Pour into ice cream canister. Freeze in ice cream maker according to manufacturer's directions; or follow refrigerator-freezer instructions on page 11.

1 serving contains:

Cal	Carb	Fat	Chol	Calcium
172	26g	8g	27mg	19mg

Plum-Orange Sorbet

ITS BEAUTIFUL COLOR AND FRESH TASTE WILL DRAW COMPLIMENTS EVERY TIME YOU MAKE IT.

Makes about 1 quart

- ⅓ cup sugar
- ⅓ cup light corn syrup
- 1 teaspoon grated orange peel
- ½ cup water
- ½ cup orange juice
- 6 fresh ripe red plums, pitted, quartered

IN A SMALL SAUCEPAN, combine sugar, corn syrup, orange peel, and water. Stir over medium heat until sugar dissolves. Stir in orange juice. Cool to room temperature. In blender or food processor fitted with a metal blade, purée plums. Place a fine strainer over a small bowl. Pour purée through strainer to remove peel, if desired. Stir strained purée into syrup mixture. Pour into ice cream canister. Freeze in ice cream maker according to manufacturer's directions; or follow refrigerator-freezer instructions on page 11.

1 serving contains:

Cal	Carb	Fat	Chol	Calcium
104	27g	0g	0mg	11mg

Spicy Plum Frozen Yogurt

TO MAKE A SPICE BAG EASILY, CUT A 6-INCH SQUARE OF CHEESECLOTH.
PLACE WHOLE SPICES IN CENTER; PULL UP SIDES AND CORNERS UNTIL
THEY MEET IN CENTER. TIE WITH STRING.

Makes about 1 quart

- 1 (3-inch) stick cinnamon, halved crosswise
- 6 whole cloves
- 6 whole allspice
- ½ cup unsweetened white grape juice
- ¼ cup water
- 1 teaspoon unflavored gelatin
- 4 medium plums, seeded and quartered
- ½ cup sugar
- 1 cup plain low-fat yogurt, stirred

TIE CINNAMON, CLOVES, AND ALLSPICE in cheesecloth. In a medium saucepan, combine spice bag with grape juice. Simmer, covered, 5 minutes. Combine water and gelatin; let stand 1 minute to soften. Remove and discard spice bag from hot grape juice; immediately stir in softened gelatin. In blender or food processor fitted with a metal blade, combine plums and sugar; process until plums are finely chopped. Add to grape juice mixture; cool. Stir in yogurt. Freeze in ice cream maker according to manufacturer's directions; or follow refrigerator-freezer instructions on page 11.

1 serving contains:

Cal	Carb	Fat	Chol	Calcium
124	27g	1g	2mg	79mg

Pomegranate Granita

ITS SPECTACULAR COLOR AND TASTE GUARANTEE UNIVERSAL APPEAL.

Makes about 1 quart

- 1½ **cups water**
- ⅓ **cup sugar**
- ⅓ **cup light corn syrup**
- 3 **fresh medium pomegranates**
- 2 **tablespoons lemon juice**

IN A SMALL SAUCEPAN, combine water, sugar, and corn syrup. Stir over medium heat until sugar dissolves; set aside. Cool to room temperature. Cut pomegranates in half crosswise. Press and turn on an orange reamer to remove juice. Reserve juice; discard pulp, seeds, and peel. There will be about 1 cup pomegranate juice. Stir pomegranate juice and lemon juice into cooled syrup. Pour into ice cream canister. Freeze in ice cream maker according to manufacturer's directions; or follow refrigerator-freezer instructions on page 11.

1 serving contains:

Cal	Carb	Fat	Chol	Calcium
148	39g	0g	0mg	5mg

Fresh Pomegranate Frozen Yogurt

FRESH BRIGHT RED POMEGRANATES ARE FILLED WITH SEEDS THAT ARE COATED WITH VERY JUICY, CRIMSON PULP.

| Makes about 1 quart |

- 2 whole fresh pomegranates (8- to 10-ounces each)
- 1 cup low-fat milk
- 1 teaspoon unflavored gelatin
- ¼ cup sugar
- ⅓ cup corn syrup
- 1 cup plain low-fat yogurt, stirred

CUT POMEGRANATE IN HALF, crosswise. Remove juice with a citrus juicer; strain and discard seeds. In a medium saucepan, combine milk and gelatin; let stand 1 minute. Stir in sugar and corn syrup. Cook and stir over low heat until gelatin dissolves. Remove from heat; cool. Add yogurt and pomegranate juice. Freeze in ice cream maker according to manufacturer's directions; or follow refrigerator-freezer instructions on page 11.

1 serving contains:

Cal	Carb	Fat	Chol	Calcium
163	36g	1g	4mg	127mg

Persimmon Frozen Yogurt

HACHIYA, A FIG-SHAPED PERSIMMON, HAS A BRIGHT GOLDEN-ORANGE COLOR AND SHOULD NOT BE USED UNTIL IT IS VERY SOFT. THE TOMATO-SHAPE FUYU IS REDDISH ORANGE AND MAY BE USED WHEN SOFT BUT SLIGHTLY FIRM. PERSIMMONS ARE AVAILABLE FROM OCTOBER TO FEBRUARY.

Makes about 1 quart

- 2 large or 3 small ripe persimmons, peeled and seeded
- 1 teaspoon lemon juice
- ½ cup sugar
- 2 tablespoons light corn syrup
- 1 teaspoon unflavored gelatin
- ¼ cup low-fat milk
- 1 cup plain low-fat yogurt, stirred

IN A BLENDER OR FOOD PROCESSOR fitted with a metal blade, purée persimmons with lemon juice, sugar, and corn syrup. In small saucepan, sprinkle gelatin over milk; let stand 1 minute. Cook and stir over low heat until gelatin dissolves. Combine with persimmon purée. Stir in yogurt. Freeze in ice cream maker according to manufacturer's directions; or follow refrigerator-freezer instructions on page 11.

1 serving contains:

Cal	Carb	Fat	Chol	Calcium
126	28g	1g	3mg	90mg

Tropical Fruits

BANANA
Bali Hai Banana Ice Cream
Tropical Ice Cream
Banana-Orange Sorbet
Trade Winds Fruit Sorbet
Banana-Macadamia Frozen Yogurt
Classic Banana Frozen Yogurt

COCONUT
Coconut Cream-Pineapple Frozen
  Yogurt
Coconut Custard Frozen Yogurt

DATE
Oasis Date Frozen Yogurt

KIWI
Kiwi Ice Cream
Kiwi Sorbet
Kiwi-Lime Frozen Yogurt
Orange-Kiwi Frozen Yogurt

MANGO
Mango Ice Cream
Mango Sorbet
Mango-Apricot Frozen Yogurt

PAPAYA
Papaya Ice Cream
Papaya Frozen Yogurt
Papaya-Nut Frozen Yogurt

PASSION FRUIT
Passion Fruit Ice Cream
Passion Fruit Frozen Yogurt

PINEAPPLE
Pineapple Tropical Frozen Yogurt
Piña Colada Frozen Yogurt

Bali Hai Banana Ice Cream

ENJOY THIS FROZEN BEAUTY FROM THE TROPICS ON ANY HOT DAY.

Makes about 2 quarts

1	large banana, peeled, cut into chunks
1	tablespoon lemon juice
2	eggs, beaten
$\frac{1}{2}$	cup sugar
1	cup pineapple juice
$1\frac{1}{2}$	cups half-and-half or whipping cream
$\frac{1}{3}$	cup flaked coconut
$\frac{1}{8}$	teaspoon almond extract

IN A BLENDER OR FOOD PROCESSOR fitted with a metal blade, purée banana and lemon juice. In a medium saucepan, combine beaten eggs, sugar, pineapple juice, and half-and-half or whipping cream. Cook and stir over low heat until slightly thickened. Stir in puréed banana, coconut, and almond extract. Pour into ice cream canister. Freeze in ice cream maker according to manufacturer's directions; or follow refrigerator-freezer instructions on page 11.

1 serving contains:

Cal	Carb	Fat	Chol	Calcium
116	16g	5g	47mg	41mg

Tropical Ice Cream

INGREDIENTS ARE AVAILABLE YEAR-ROUND, SO MAKE THIS ANYTIME.

Makes about 1½ quarts

- 3 medium bananas, peeled, mashed
- 1 (6-ounce) can orange-juice concentrate, partially thawed
- 1 (8-ounce) can crushed pineapple with juice
- 2 tablespoons lemon juice
- ¼ cup sugar
- ½ teaspoon vanilla extract
- ½ cup half-and-half

IN A BOWL combine bananas, orange-juice concentrate, pineapple with juice, lemon juice, sugar, and vanilla. Stir in half-and-half. Pour into ice cream canister. Freeze in ice cream maker according to manufacturer's directions; or follow refrigerator-freezer instructions on page 11.

1 serving contains:

Cal	Carb	Fat	Chol	Calcium
119	26g	2g	5mg	27mg

Banana-Orange Sorbet

LIKE MOST SORBETS, THIS ONE IS AT ITS BEST WHEN EATEN AS SOON AS IT IS FROZEN.

Makes about 2 quarts

- ⅔ cup sugar
- ⅔ cup light corn syrup
- 1 cup water
- 2 cups orange juice
- 4 large ripe bananas, peeled, cut in pieces
- ¼ cup orange liqueur, if desired

IN A SMALL SAUCEPAN, combine sugar, corn syrup, and water. Stir over low heat until sugar dissolves. Stir in orange juice; set aside. Purée bananas in blender or food processor fitted with a metal blade. Stir into juice mixture. Add liqueur, if desired. Pour into ice cream canister. Freeze in ice cream maker according to manufacturer's directions; or follow refrigerator-freezer instructions on page 11.

1 serving contains:

Cal	Carb	Fat	Chol	Calcium
155	40g	0g	0mg	8mg

Trade Winds Fruit Sorbet

FOR A COOL SUMMER LUNCH, SPOON THIS DELIGHTFUL COMBINATION ONTO MIXED GREENS AND ENJOY A SORBET SALAD.

Makes about 1½ quarts

- 2 bananas, peeled, mashed
- 2 (12-ounce) cans apricot nectar (3 cups)
- ¼ cup lime juice
- 2 (6-ounce) cans pineapple juice (1½ cups)
- 1 cup sugar

IN A LARGE BOWL, combine bananas and apricot nectar. Stir in lime juice, pineapple juice, and sugar. Pour into ice cream canister. Freeze in ice cream maker according to manufacturer's directions; or follow refrigerator-freezer instructions on page 11.

1 serving contains:

Cal	Carb	Fat	Chol	Calcium
164	42g	0g	0mg	14mg

Banana-Macadamia Frozen Yogurt

TROPICAL FRUITS AND NUTS GO NATURALLY TOGETHER. IMAGINE YOU'RE ON A PLANTATION IN HAWAII.

Makes about 1 quart

- ½ cup low-fat milk
- 1 teaspoon unflavored gelatin
- 2 medium bananas, peeled and quartered
- 2 tablespoons light corn syrup
- ½ cup sugar
- 1 teaspoon lemon juice
- ½ teaspoon vanilla extract
- 1 cup plain low-fat yogurt, stirred
- ¼ cup chopped macadamia nuts

IN A SMALL SAUCEPAN, combine milk and gelatin; let stand one minute. Stir over low heat until gelatin dissolves; set aside. In blender or food processor fitted with a metal blade, combine bananas, corn syrup, sugar, lemon juice, and vanilla. Process until bananas are puréed. Combine with dissolved gelatin, yogurt, and macadamia nuts. Freeze in ice cream maker according to manufacturer's directions; or follow refrigerator-freezer instructions on page 11 and stir in nuts after final processing or beating.

1 serving contains:

Cal	Carb	Fat	Chol	Calcium
196	36g	5g	3mg	107mg

Classic Banana Frozen Yogurt

TRY TOPPING A SCOOP OF THIS WITH A DRIZZLE OF CHOCOLATE OR RASPBERRY SYRUP.

Makes about 1 quart

- 2 medium bananas, peeled and quartered
- ½ cup sugar
- 2 tablespoons honey
- 1 tablespoon lemon juice
- ½ cup low-fat milk
- 1 cup plain low-fat yogurt, stirred

IN A BLENDER OR FOOD PROCESSOR fitted with a metal blade, combine bananas, sugar, honey, and lemon juice. Process until bananas are puréed. Stir in milk and yogurt. Freeze in ice cream maker according to manufacturer's directions; or follow refrigerator-freezer instructions on page 11.

1 serving contains:

Cal	Carb	Fat	Chol	Calcium
157	36g	1g	3mg	103mg

Coconut Cream-Pineapple Frozen Yogurt

IF YOU HAVE A SWEET TOOTH, YOU'LL LOVE THIS. IT'S QUITE SMOOTH AND RICH-TASTING—SLIGHTLY SWEETER THAN MOST FROZEN YOGURTS.

Makes about 1 quart

- 1 (8-ounce) can crushed pineapple in unsweetened juice
- 1 (16-ounce) can cream of coconut
- 1 tablespoon rum or rum flavoring
- 1 cup plain low-fat yogurt, stirred

IN A MEDIUM BOWL, combine pineapple with juice, cream of coconut, rum or rum flavoring, and plain low-fat yogurt. Freeze in ice cream maker according to manufacturer's directions; or follow refrigerator-freezer instructions on page 11.

1 serving contains:

Cal	Carb	Fat	Chol	Calcium
241	16g	18g	2mg	82mg

Coconut Custard Frozen Yogurt

A DELICIOUS BLEND OF INGREDIENTS BORROWED FROM COCONUT PIE.

Makes about 1 quart

- 1 cup flaked coconut
- 1 cup low-fat milk
- 1 egg, slightly beaten
- ½ cup sugar
- ½ teaspoon vanilla extract
- 2 cups vanilla low-fat yogurt, stirred

IN A BLENDER OR FOOD PROCESSOR fitted with a metal blade, combine coconut and milk. Process until coconut is finely chopped. In a small saucepan, combine with beaten egg and sugar. Cook and stir over moderate heat until thickened. Strain; discard pieces of coconut; cool. Stir in vanilla and yogurt. Freeze in ice cream maker according to manufacturer's directions; or follow refrigerator-freezer instructions on page 11.

1 serving contains:

Cal	Carb	Fat	Chol	Calcium
223	36g	6g	41mg	196mg

Oasis Date Frozen Yogurt

NATURALLY SWEET DATES PROVIDE A DELICIOUS CONTRAST TO THE SLIGHTLY TART ORANGE YOGURT.

Makes about 1 quart

2	teaspoons cornstarch
¼	cup sugar
1	cup milk
2	tablespoons honey
½	teaspoon grated orange peel
¾	cup finely chopped dates
2	cups low-fat orange yogurt, stirred

IN A MEDIUM SAUCEPAN, combine cornstarch and sugar; stir in milk, honey, and orange peel. Cook and stir over moderate heat until orange peel is translucent (about 5 minutes). Remove from heat. Add dates; cool. Stir in yogurt. Freeze in ice cream maker according to manufacturer's directions; or follow refrigerator-freezer instructions on page 11.

1 serving contains:

Cal	Carb	Fat	Chol	Calcium
213	45g	2g	10mg	196mg

Kiwi Ice Cream

IN NEW ZEALAND, THESE BEAUTIES ARE CALLED CHINESE GOOSEBERRIES. FOR MAXIMUM FLAVOR, MAKE SURE THE KIWI FRUIT IS RIPE.

Makes about 1 quart

2	ripe kiwis, peeled, quartered
$\frac{1}{3}$	cup orange juice
2	eggs, beaten
$1\frac{1}{2}$	cups sugar
$1\frac{1}{2}$	cups half-and-half or whipping cream
$\frac{1}{2}$	teaspoon vanilla extract
6 to 8	drops green food coloring

IN A BLENDER OR FOOD PROCESSOR fitted with a metal blade, purée kiwis and orange juice; set aside. In a medium saucepan, combine beaten eggs, sugar, and half-and-half or whipping cream. Cook and stir over low heat until thickened. Stir in kiwi mixture, vanilla, and food coloring. Pour into ice cream canister. Freeze in ice cream maker according to manufacturer's directions; or follow refrigerator-freezer instructions on page 11.

1 serving contains:

Cal	Carb	Fat	Chol	Calcium
321	58g	9g	93mg	83mg

Kiwi Sorbet

SERVE THIS DELIGHTFULLY REFRESHING, PALE GREEN SORBET ON ANY OCCASION.

Makes about 2 quarts

- 1 cup sugar
- 1 cup light corn syrup
- 2 cups water
- 6 ripe kiwis, peeled and quartered
- ¼ cup lemon juice

IN A MEDIUM SAUCEPAN, combine sugar, corn syrup, and water. Stir over medium heat until sugar dissolves; set aside. In blender or food processor fitted with a metal blade, purée kiwis and lemon juice. Stir into syrup. Pour into ice cream canister. Freeze in ice cream maker according to manufacturer's directions; or follow refrigerator-freezer instructions on page 11.

1 serving contains:

Cal	Carb	Fat	Chol	Calcium
168	44g	0g	0mg	17mg

Kiwi-Lime Frozen Yogurt

PROPERLY RIPENED KIWI FRUIT FEELS QUITE SOFT WHEN ITS SKIN IS PRESSED.

| Makes about 1 quart |

- **2** ripe kiwis, peeled and quartered
- **4** teaspoons lime juice
- **¾** cup sugar
- **½** teaspoon vanilla extract
- **1** cup low-fat milk
- **1** cup plain low-fat yogurt, stirred
- **3 or 4** drops green food coloring
- **¼** cup chopped pistachios

IN A BLENDER OR FOOD PROCESSOR fitted with a metal blade, combine kiwi, lime juice, sugar, and vanilla. Process until almost smooth. In medium bowl, combine puréed mixture, milk, yogurt, food coloring, and pistachios. Stir until well blended. If you wish to remove the seeds, strain the mixture at this point. Freeze in ice cream maker according to manufacturer's directions; or follow refrigerator-freezer instructions on page 11.

1 serving contains:

Cal	Carb	Fat	Chol	Calcium
189	35g	4g	4mg	143mg

Orange-Kiwi Frozen Yogurt

THE DELICATE FLAVOR OF KIWI IS COMPLIMENTED BY ORANGE. THIS REFRESHING COMBINATION OF FLAVORS MAKES AN IDEAL DESSERT FOR ENTERTAINING.

Makes about 1 quart

¾	cup sugar
1	egg
1	cup low-fat milk
2	ripe kiwis, peeled
⅓	cup orange juice
¼	teaspoon vanilla extract
3 or 4	drops green food coloring, optional
1	cup plain low-fat yogurt

IN A SMALL SAUCEPAN, combine sugar and egg; beat until well blended. Add milk; cook, stirring frequently, over medium-low heat 10 to 15 minutes or until mixture thickens and coats a metal spoon. Remove from heat; cool. In blender or food processor, purée kiwi with orange juice. Add puréed kiwi, vanilla, food coloring (if desired), and yogurt to cooled egg mixture. If you wish to remove the seeds, strain the mixture at this point. Freeze in ice cream maker according to manufacturer's directions; or follow refrigerator-freezer instructions on page 11.

1 serving contains:

Cal	Carb	Fat	Chol	Calcium
175	35g	2g	40mg	140mg

Mango Ice Cream

RIPE MANGOES HAVE A DELIGHTFUL AROMA THAT GUARANTEES GREAT FLAVOR.

Makes about 1 quart

    1 mango
    1 tablespoon lemon juice
    2 teaspoons cornstarch
  ⅓ cup sugar
1½ cups half-and-half
    1 egg yolk, beaten
    2 tablespoons light corn syrup

PEEL MANGO. Cut pulp from seed; discard seed. In blender or food processor fitted with a metal blade, purée mango pulp with lemon juice. In medium saucepan, combine cornstarch and sugar. Stir in half-and-half, beaten egg yolk, and corn syrup. Cook and stir over medium heat until bubbly; cook 1 minute longer. Cool. Stir in puréed mango. Pour into ice cream canister. Freeze in ice cream maker according to manufacturer's directions; or follow refrigerator-freezer instructions on page 11.

1 serving contains:

Cal	Carb	Fat	Chol	Calcium
177	26g	8g	58mg	71mg

Mango Sorbet

REFRESHING AS A TRADE-WIND BREEZE.

Makes about 2 quarts

3	cups water
⅔	cup sugar
⅔	cup light corn syrup
2	large ripe mangoes
1	cup orange juice
¼	cup orange liqueur

IN A MEDIUM SAUCEPAN, combine water, sugar, and corn syrup. Stir over medium heat until sugar dissolves; set aside to cool. Peel mangoes. Cut pulp from seeds; discard seeds. In blender or food processor fitted with a metal blade, purée mango pulp and orange juice. Stir into cooled syrup. Add liqueur. Pour into ice cream canister. Freeze in ice cream maker according to manufacturer's directions; or follow refrigerator-freezer instructions on page 11.

1 serving contains:

Cal	Carb	Fat	Chol	Calcium
133	35g	0g	0mg	8mg

Mango-Apricot Frozen Yogurt

RIPE MANGOES HAVE A WONDERFUL AROMA. CHOOSE FRUIT THAT GIVES EASILY WHEN LIGHTLY PRESSED WITH FINGERS.

Makes about 1 quart

- 2 medium mangoes, peeled and cubed
- ½ cup apricot-pineapple juice
- ⅓ cup sugar
- ⅛ teaspoon ground mace
- ¾ cup plain low-fat yogurt, stirred

MANGO PULP CLINGS to a large seed in the center of the fruit. Slice strips of pulp away from the seed; then cut pulp crosswise into small cubes.

In a blender or food processor fitted with a metal blade, combine mangoes, apricot-pineapple juice, and sugar. Purée until smooth. Stir in ground mace and yogurt. Freeze in ice cream maker according to manufacturer's directions; or follow refrigerator-freezer instructions on page 11.

1 serving contains:

Cal	Carb	Fat	Chol	Calcium
118	28g	1g	2mg	64mg

Papaya Ice Cream

BRING THE FLAVOR OF HAWAII TO YOUR TABLE.

Makes about 1 quart

- 1 ripe papaya, peeled, seeded, sliced
- 1 tablespoon lemon juice
- ¾ cup sugar
- 2 eggs, beaten
- 1 cup milk
- 1 cup half-and-half or whipping cream

IN A BLENDER OR FOOD PROCESSOR fitted with a metal blade, purée papaya and lemon juice. In a medium saucepan, combine sugar, beaten eggs, and milk. Cook and stir over low heat until mixture thickens and coats a spoon. Add puréed papaya and half-and-half or whipping cream. Pour into ice cream canister. Freeze in ice cream maker according to manufacturer's directions; or follow refrigerator-freezer instructions on page 11.

1 serving contains:

Cal	Carb	Fat	Chol	Calcium
219	34g	8g	91mg	11mg

Papaya Frozen Yogurt

HONEY COMBINED WITH LIME JUICE ADDS JUST THE RIGHT AMOUNT OF ZEST TO THIS REFRESHING FROZEN DESSERT.

| Makes about 1 quart |

- ½ cup low-fat milk
- 1 teaspoon unflavored gelatin
- 1 large ripe papaya, peeled, seeded, and cubes (about 1 pound)
- ½ cup sugar
- 2 tablespoons honey
- 1 tablespoon lime juice
- 1½ cups plain low-fat yogurt, stirred

IN A SMALL SAUCEPAN, combine milk and gelatin; let stand 1 minute. Stir over low heat until gelatin dissolves; set aside. In blender or food processor fitted with a metal blade, purée papaya, sugar, honey, and lime juice until almost smooth. Combine papaya purée, gelatin mixture, and yogurt. Freeze in ice cream maker according to manufacturer's directions; or follow refrigerator-freezer instructions on page 11.

1 serving contains:

Cal	Carb	Fat	Chol	Calcium
160	34g	1g	5mg	153mg

Papaya-Nut Frozen Yogurt

COLOR, TEXTURE, AND FLAVOR ARE ALL PRESENT TO CREATE AN UNUSUAL DESSERT.

Makes about 1 quart

½	cup low-fat milk
2	slices raisin or cinnamon bread, quartered
½	teaspoon ground cardamom
½	cup sugar
½	teaspoon grated orange peel
1	cup chopped and seeded cantaloupe or Crenshaw melon
1	small papaya, peeled, seeded, and chopped
½	cup toasted slivered almonds
¾	cup plain low-fat yogurt

IN A FOOD PROCESSOR fitted with a metal blade, combine milk, bread, cardamom, sugar, and orange peel; process briefly. Add chopped cantaloupe or Crenshaw melon, papaya, and toasted almonds. Process until fruit is finely chopped but not puréed. Stir in yogurt. Freeze in ice cream maker according to manufacturer's directions; or follow refrigerator-freezer instructions on page 11.

1 serving contains:

Cal	Carb	Fat	Chol	Calcium
200	31g	7g	3mg	126mg

Passion Fruit Ice Cream

THIS EGG-SHAPED TROPICAL FRUIT IMPARTS A WONDERFUL TART-SWEET TASTE TO ICE CREAM.

Makes about 1 quart

1	teaspoon unflavored gelatin
½	cup low-fat milk
4	passion fruit
⅓	cup sugar
2	tablespoons light corn syrup
2	teaspoons lemon juice
1	cup half-and-half
½	cup whipping cream

IN A SMALL SAUCEPAN, sprinkle gelatin over milk; let stand 1 minute. Stir over low heat until gelatin dissolves. Remove from heat; set aside. Cut each passion fruit in half crosswise. Scoop out pulp and seeds; discard rind. In blender or food processor fitted with a metal blade, purée pulp and seeds. Strain juice; discard seeds. Combine passion-fruit juice with milk mixture, sugar, corn syrup, lemon juice, half-and-half, and whipping cream. Pour into ice cream canister. Freeze in ice cream maker according to manufacturer's directions; or follow refrigerator-freezer instructions on page 11.

1 serving contains:

Cal	Carb	Fat	Chol	Calcium
205	23g	12g	43mg	82mg

Passion Fruit Frozen Yogurt

READY-TO-EAT FRESH PASSION FRUIT IS A STRANGE-LOOKING EGG-SHAPED TROPICAL FRUIT FROM NEW ZEALAND WITH A WONDERFUL TART-SWEET FLAVOR.

Makes about 1 quart

- ½ cup low-fat milk
- 1 teaspoon unflavored gelatin
- 5 passion fruits
- ¾ cup sugar
- 1 teaspoon lemon juice
- 1½ cups plain low-fat yogurt, stirred
- 1 egg white
- ⅓ cup water
- ⅓ cup fat-free dry milk

IN A SMALL SAUCEPAN, combine milk and gelatin; let stand 1 minute. Cook and stir over low heat until gelatin dissolves; set aside. Cut each passion fruit in half crosswise; scoop out pulp and seeds. Discard shell. In blender or food processor fitted with a metal blade, purée pulp and seeds. Strain; discard seeds. Combine passion fruit juice with sugar, lemon juice, and dissolved gelatin. Stir in yogurt. In medium bowl, combine egg white, water, and fat-free dry milk. Beat until stiff but not dry. Fold into yogurt mixture. Freeze in ice cream maker according to manufacturer's directions; or follow refrigerator-freezer instructions on page 11.

1 serving contains:

Cal	Carb	Fat	Chol	Calcium
176	36g	1g	5mg	191mg

Pineapple Tropical Frozen Yogurt

IT'S EASY TO CREATE AN EXCITING EXOTIC DESSERT WITH ALL THE TROPICAL FRUITS AVAILABLE IN YOUR MARKET.

Makes about 1 quart

- 1 (8-ounce) can crushed pineapple in unsweetened juice
- 1 teaspoon unflavored gelatin
- 1 small papaya, peeled, seeded, and cut into chunks
- 1 small banana, peeled and cut into chunks
- ½ cup sugar
- 2 tablespoons honey
- 1 cup plain low-fat yogurt, stirred

IN A SMALL SAUCEPAN, combine pineapple and gelatin; let stand 1 minute. Cook and stir over low heat until gelatin dissolves; set aside. In a blender or food processor fitted with a metal blade, combine papaya, banana, sugar, and honey. Process until fruit is finely chopped. Combine with pineapple mixture. Stir in yogurt. Freeze in ice cream maker according to manufacturer's directions; or follow refrigerator-freezer instructions on page 11.

1 serving contains:

Cal	Carb	Fat	Chol	Calcium
157	36g	1g	2mg	89mg

Piña Colada Frozen Yogurt

THIS IS REMINISCENT OF EXOTIC FRESH-FRUIT CONCOCTIONS FROM THE CARIBBEAN.

Makes about 1 quart

- 1 banana, peeled and quartered
- 2 cups ripe fresh pineapple chunks
- ¼ cup flaked coconut
- ½ cup brown sugar
- 2 tablespoons rum or rum flavoring
- 1 cup vanilla low-fat yogurt, stirred

IN A BLENDER OR FOOD PROCESSOR fitted with a metal blade, combine banana, pineapple, and coconut. Blend until almost smooth. Add brown sugar and rum or rum flavoring. Stir in yogurt. Freeze in ice cream maker according to manufacturer's directions; or follow refrigerator-freezer instructions on page 11.

1 serving contains:

Cal	Carb	Fat	Chol	Calcium
175	36g	2g	2mg	91mg

Melons, Exotic Fruits, and Vegetables

CANTALOUPE
Cantaloupe Sherbet
Cantaloupe-Wine Sorbet
Ginger-Honey-Cantaloupe Frozen
  Yogurt

HONEYDEW
Minted Honeydew Ice Cream
Honeydew-Melon Ice
Melon-Raspberry Sorbet

GRAPE
Grape Punch Sorbet
Concord Grape Frozen Yogurt
Lemon-Grape Frozen Yogurt

PUMPKIN
Pumpkin Ice Cream
Pumpkin-Orange Frozen Yogurt

RHUBARB
Rhubarb Custard Ice Cream

WATERMELON
Watermelon Granita
Watermelon-Wine Sorbet
Watermelon Punch Frozen Yogurt

MIXED VEGETABLE
Green Chowder Frappé
Gazpacho Frappé

Cantaloupe Sherbet

THE PERFECT ENDING TO A BACKYARD BARBECUE. FOR ADDED COLOR, TOP WITH FRESH BLUEBERRIES.

Makes about 2 quarts

1	medium cantaloupe, peeled, seeded, cubed
2	tablespoons lemon juice
½	cup sugar
¼	cup honey
3	cups milk
½	teaspoon vanilla extract

IN A BLENDER OR FOOD PROCESSOR fitted with a metal blade, purée cantaloupe and lemon juice. In a large bowl, combine sugar, honey, and milk. Add puréed cantaloupe mixture and vanilla. Stir until sugar dissolves. Pour into ice cream canister. Freeze in ice cream maker according to manufacturer's directions; or follow refrigerator-freezer instructions on page 11.

1 serving contains:

Cal	Carb	Fat	Chol	Calcium
108	21g	2g	8mg	78mg

Cantaloupe-Wine Sorbet

VARY THIS RECIPE BY USING YOUR FAVORITE SWEET WINE.

| Makes about 2 quarts |

- ½ cup sugar
- ¼ cup light corn syrup
- ¾ cup water
- 1 large ripe cantaloupe or Crenshaw melon, peeled, seeded, cubed
- 1 tablespoon lemon juice
- 1 cup sauterne wine

IN A SMALL SAUCEPAN, combine sugar, corn syrup, and water. Stir over low heat until sugar dissolves; cool to room temperature. In blender or food processor fitted with a metal blade, purée melon and lemon juice until smooth. In a medium bowl, combine purée, cooled syrup, and wine. Pour into ice cream canister. Freeze in ice cream maker according to manufacturer's directions; or follow refrigerator-freezer instructions on page 11.

1 serving contains:

Cal	Carb	Fat	Chol	Calcium
88	20g	0g	0mg	11mg

Ginger-Honey-Cantaloupe Frozen Yogurt

FRESHLY GRATED GINGER BRINGS OUT THE BEST IN THIS CANTALOUPE-ORANGE COMBINATION.

Makes about 1 quart

- 2 cups cubed and seeded cantaloupe
- 1 teaspoon grated fresh ginger
- ½ teaspoon grated orange peel
- 2 tablespoons honey
- ½ cup sugar
- 1 teaspoon unflavored gelatin
- ½ cup orange juice
- 1 cup plain low-fat yogurt

IN A BLENDER OR FOOD PROCESSOR fitted with a metal blade, combine cantaloupe, ginger, orange peel, honey, and sugar. Process until puréed. In a small saucepan sprinkle gelatin over orange juice; let stand 1 minute. Cook and stir over low heat until gelatin dissolves. Add to puréed fruit mixture. Stir in yogurt. Freeze in ice cream maker according to manufacturer's directions; or follow refrigerator-freezer instructions on page 11.

1 serving contains:

Cal	Carb	Fat	Chol	Calcium
142	32g	1g	2mg	84mg

Minted Honeydew Ice Cream

COOL MINT FLAVOR COMPLEMENTS HONEYDEW MELON.

Makes about 1 quart

- ¼ cup water
- 1 teaspoon unflavored gelatin
- 1 tablespoon coarsely chopped fresh mint leaves
- 2 tablespoons lemon juice
- 2 tablespoons light corn syrup
- ⅓ cup sugar
- 2 cups honeydew melon cubes
- 1 cup milk or half-and-half

IN A SMALL SAUCEPAN, combine water and gelatin; let stand 1 minute. Add mint, lemon juice, corn syrup, and sugar; cook over low heat until gelatin dissolves. Remove from heat. Cover and let stand at least 1 hour. Strain; discard mint leaves. In blender or food processor fitted with a metal blade, purée honeydew. Combine with strained-mint mixture and milk or half-and-half. Pour into ice cream canister. Freeze in ice cream maker according to manufacturer's directions; or follow refrigerator-freezer instructions on page 11.

1 serving contains:

Cal	Carb	Fat	Chol	Calcium
109	24g	1g	6mg	53mg

Honeydew-Melon Ice

MIDSUMMER BLUE-RIBBON WINNER.

Makes about 2 quarts

1½ cups sugar

1½ cups water

1 medium honeydew

2 teaspoons lime juice

IN A MEDIUM SAUCEPAN, combine sugar and water. Stir over medium heat until sugar dissolves. Stirring occasionally, cook to 234F (112C) on a candy thermometer or until syrup spins a 2-inch thread when slowly poured from a spoon. Set aside to cool at room temperature for 10 minutes. Cut melon from rind; remove and discard seeds. Cut fruit into 1-inch cubes. Purée melon cubes and lime juice in blender or food processor until almost smooth. Stir purée into reserved syrup. Pour into ice cream canister. Freeze in ice cream maker according to manufacturer's directions.

Freezer method: Pour prepared mixture into a 9-inch square pan or several undivided ice trays. Cover with foil or plastic wrap. Place in freezer; freeze until firm, 3 to 6 hours. Scrape frozen mixture with a fork until pieces resemble finely crushed ice. For a smoother texture, freeze prepared mixture until firm; break into small pieces. Spoon half of mixture into chilled food processor bowl. Beat with metal blade until light and fluffy but not thawed. Repeat with remaining frozen mixture. Serve immediately or return beaten mixture to pan and freeze until firm, 1 to 3 hours.

1 serving contains:

Cal	Carb	Fat	Chol	Calcium
139	36g	0g	0mg	1mg

Melon-Raspberry Sorbet

WHAT COULD BE EASIER? CREATE THIS DELICIOUS TREAT WITH JUST THREE INGREDIENTS.

Makes about 2 quarts

2 cups fresh or frozen raspberries, thawed

1 large ripe honeydew melon, peeled, cubed

¼ cup sugar

PURÉE RASPBERRIES in blender or food processor fitted with a metal blade. Pour into a fine strainer. Use back of a spoon to press purée through strainer into a medium bowl; set aside. Discard seeds. Purée melon half at a time in blender or food processor fitted with a metal blade. Pour melon purée into strained raspberry purée. Add sugar; stir to blend. Pour into ice cream canister. Freeze in ice cream maker according to manufacturer's directions; or follow refrigerator-freezer instructions on page 11.

1 serving contains:

Cal	Carb	Fat	Chol	Calcium
82	21g	0g	0mg	14mg

Grape Punch Sorbet

THIS REFRESHING DESSERT MAY REMIND YOU OF A SPOONABLE FRUIT PUNCH.

Makes about 2 quarts

- 1/3 **cup sugar**
- 1/3 **cup light corn syrup**
- 2 **cups white grape juice**
- 2 **(6-ounce) cans pineapple juice (1½ cups)**
- 1 **cup orange juice**
- 1 **(12-ounce) can lemon-lime soda**

IN A MEDIUM SAUCEPAN, combine sugar, corn syrup, and white grape juice. Stir over medium heat until sugar dissolves. Stir in pineapple juice, orange juice, and lemon-lime soda. Cool to room temperature. Pour into ice cream canister. Freeze in ice cream maker according to manufacturer's directions; or follow refrigerator-freezer instructions on page 11.

1 serving contains:

Cal	Carb	Fat	Chol	Calcium
102	26g	0g	0mg	12mg

Concord Grape Frozen Yogurt

TAKE ADVANTAGE OF FRESH CONCORD GRAPES' SHORT SEASON—SEPTEMBER AND OCTOBER.

Makes about 1 quart

2	cups fresh Concord grapes
½	cup sugar
2	teaspoons cornstarch
¼	cup light corn syrup
1	cup low-fat milk
1¼	cups plain low-fat yogurt, stirred

IN A BLENDER OR FOOD PROCESSOR fitted with a metal blade, purée grapes. Strain and discard skins and seeds; set aside juice. In a small saucepan, combine sugar and cornstarch; stir in corn syrup and milk. Cook and stir over low heat 6 to 8 minutes or until mixture simmers. Stir in strained grape juice and yogurt. Freeze in ice cream maker according to manufacturer's directions; or follow refrigerator-freezer instructions on page 11.

1 serving contains:

Cal	Carb	Fat	Chol	Calcium
179	39g	2g	6mg	148mg

Lemon-Grape Frozen Yogurt

LEMON-FLAVORED YOGURT LENDS A DELICATE FLAVOR TO THIS UNIQUE GRAPE COMBINATION.

Makes about 1 quart

- ¼ cup water
- 1 teaspoon unflavored gelatin
- 1½ cups Concord grape juice
- ⅓ cup sugar
- ½ cup low-fat milk
- 1 tablespoon light corn syrup
- 1 cup low-fat lemon yogurt, stirred

IN A SMALL SAUCEPAN, combine water and gelatin; let stand 1 minute. Cook and stir over low heat until gelatin dissolves; remove from heat. In a medium bowl, combine grape juice, sugar, milk, corn syrup, and dissolved gelatin. Stir in yogurt. Freeze in ice cream maker according to manufacturer's directions; or follow refrigerator-freezer instructions on page 11.

1 serving contains:

Cal	Carb	Fat	Chol	Calcium
137	30g	1g	4mg	101mg

Rhubarb Custard Ice Cream

MILD RHUBARB FLAVOR IS ENHANCED BY THE ORANGE CUSTARD.

Makes about 1½ quarts

½	pound fresh rhubarb, cut in 1-inch pieces (about 2 cups)
¼	cup water
2	cups half-and-half
3	eggs, beaten
1¼	cups sugar
1	cup whipping cream
1	teaspoon grated orange peel
3 to 5	drops red food coloring

IN A MEDIUM SAUCEPAN, combine rhubarb and water; cover and simmer until tender, about 5 minutes. Purée in blender or food processor fitted with a metal blade; set aside. In a medium saucepan, combine half-and-half, beaten eggs, and sugar. Cook and stir over low heat until mixture thickens and coats a spoon. Stir in puréed rhubarb, whipping cream, orange peel, and food coloring. Pour into ice cream canister. Freeze in ice cream maker according to manufacturer's directions; or follow refrigerator-freezer instructions on page 11.

1 serving contains:

Cal	Carb	Fat	Chol	Calcium
269	29g	16g	114mg	95mg

Watermelon Granita

LOVELY TO LOOK AT AND DELIGHTFUL TO EAT.

Makes about 2 quarts

- ⅔ **cup sugar**
- ½ **cup water**
- ⅔ **cup light corn syrup**
- 2 **tablespoons lemon juice**
- ¼ **large watermelon**

IN A MEDIUM SAUCEPAN, combine sugar, water, and corn syrup. Stir over medium heat until mixture comes to a boil. Without stirring, simmer over low heat 5 minutes. Stir in lemon juice; cool to room temperature. Cut melon from rind, reserving only red fruit. Remove and discard seeds. Cut fruit into 1-inch cubes, making about 8 cups. Purée melon cubes about 2 cups at a time in blender or food processor fitted with a metal blade. Stir into cooled syrup. Pour into ice cream canister. Freeze in ice cream maker according to manufacturer's directions; or follow refrigerator-freezer instructions on page 11.

1 serving contains:

Cal	Carb	Fat	Chol	Calcium
132	38g	0g	0mg	10mg

Watermelon-Wine Sorbet

A SURPRISE AWAITS ALL WHO ENJOY WATERMELON—DELICATE AND REFRESHING.

Makes about 1½ quarts

- ¼ medium watermelon
- ½ cup sugar
- ⅓ cup light corn syrup
- ¼ cup port wine

CUT MELON FROM RIND, reserving only red fruit. Remove and discard seeds. Cut fruit into 1-inch cubes, making about 6 cups. Purée melon cubes about 2 cups at a time in a blender or food processor fitted with a metal blade. Pour into a medium bowl; set aside. In a small saucepan, combine sugar, corn syrup, and wine. Stir over low heat until sugar dissolves; cool to room temperature. Stir into puréed watermelon. Pour into ice cream canister. Freeze in ice cream maker according to manufacturer's directions; or follow refrigerator-freezer instructions on page 11.

1 serving contains:

Cal	Carb	Fat	Chol	Calcium
112	30g	0g	0mg	9mg

Watermelon Punch Frozen Yogurt

DO NOT ADD WATER TO THE FROZEN FRUIT PUNCH; THE CONCENTRATED JUICES PROVIDE A REFRESHING FRUIT TASTE.

Makes about 1 quart

- 1 cup cubed and seeded watermelon
- ⅓ cup sugar
- 1 teaspoon unflavored gelatin
- ¼ cup water
- 1 (6-ounce) can frozen red fruit punch concentrate, thawed
- 1 tablespoon black-raspberry liqueur, optional
- ¾ cup plain low-fat yogurt, stirred

IN A BLENDER OR FOOD PROCESSOR fitted with a metal blade, purée watermelon and sugar. In a small saucepan, sprinkle gelatin on water; let stand 1 minute. Cook and stir over low heat until gelatin dissolves. Mix with puréed melon. Add fruit punch concentrate and liqueur, if desired. Stir in yogurt. Freeze in ice cream maker according to manufacturer's directions; or follow refrigerator-freezer instructions on page 11.

1 serving contains:

Cal	Carb	Fat	Chol	Calcium
130	28g	1g	2mg	64mg

Green Chowder Frappé

PERFECT FIRST-COURSE DISH FOR SUMMER ENTERTAINING.

Makes 6 servings

3 green onions, chopped

½ cup watercress leaves

1 cup fresh or frozen peas, thawed

2 cups chicken broth or bouillon

1 potato, peeled, chopped

½ teaspoon salt

⅛ teaspoon pepper

¼ teaspoon seasoned salt

½ cup dairy sour cream

Sour cream for garnish

IN A LARGE SAUCEPAN, combine green onions, watercress, peas, broth or bouillon, potato, salt, pepper, and seasoned salt. Bring to a boil over medium heat. Cover and simmer over low heat until vegetables are tender. Pour into blender or food processor fitted with a metal blade. Purée; pour into a large bowl; cool to room temperature. Stir in sour cream. Pour into a 9" 3 5" loaf pan or several undivided ice trays. Cover with foil or plastic wrap. Place in freezer; freeze until slushy, 1 to 3 hours. Spoon into sherbet glasses or champagne glasses. Garnish top with sour cream. Serve immediately. If mixture freezes solid, scrape with a fork until pieces resemble finely crushed ice. Serve immediately.

1 serving contains:

Cal	Carb	Fat	Chol	Calcium
95	10g	5g	9mg	39mg

Gazpacho Frappé

SERVE THIS SAVORY FRAPPÉ AS THE FIRST COURSE OF A MEXICAN
DINNER.

| Makes 6 servings |

4	green onions, cut in ½-inch lengths
1	medium cucumber, peeled, seeded, cubed
½	green pepper, coarsely chopped
4	ripe tomatoes, coarsely chopped
½	teaspoon salt
¼	teaspoon garlic salt
⅛	teaspoon paprika
⅛	teaspoon black pepper
1	cup beef broth or bouillon

IN A BLENDER OR FOOD PROCESSOR fitted with a metal blade, combine green onion pieces, cucumber, green pepper, and tomatoes. Blend until mixture is in very small pieces. In a large bowl, combine puréed mixture, salt, garlic salt, paprika, black pepper, and broth or bouillon. Pour into ice cream canister. Freeze until slushy. If mixture freezes solid, scrape with a fork until pieces resemble finely crushed ice. Spoon into sherbet glasses or champagne glasses. Serve immediately.

1 serving contains:

Cal	Carb	Fat	Chol	Calcium
36	7g	0g	0mg	18mg

Nuts and Candies

PECAN

Butter-Pecan Ice Cream

Pecan-Chocolate Crunch Ice Cream

Pecan-Butterscotch Ripple Ice
Cream

Maple-Pecan Frozen Yogurt

MACADAMIA

Coconut-Macadamia Ice Cream

White Chocolate-Macadamia
Frozen Yogurt

MISCELLANEOUS NUTS

Hazelnut Gelato

Alpine-Peanut Ice Cream

Walnut-Maple Ice Cream

CANDY

Snickers® Candy Ice Cream

Toffee-Coffee Ice Cream

Licorice-Stick Ice Cream

Peppermint-Stick Ice Cream

Peppermint Frozen Yogurt

Oreo® Cookie Frozen Yogurt

Butterfinger® Frozen Yogurt

Peanut-Butter Cups Frozen Yogurt

Peanut Butter-Caramel Frozen
Yogurt

Grasshopper Frozen Yogurt

Crunchy Toffee Bar Frozen Yogurt

Chocolate-Mint Parfait Frozen
Yogurt

Pastel Mint Frozen Yogurt

Burnt Sugar Frozen Yogurt

Butterscotch Frozen Yogurt

Butter-Pecan Ice Cream

FANTASTIC FLAVOR! OUR FAVORITE ICE CREAM FOR CHOCOLATE SUNDAES.

Makes about 1 quart

⅓	cup coarsely chopped pecans
1	tablespoon butter
1	cup packed brown sugar
2	eggs, beaten
1½	cups half-and-half
½	cup whipping cream
1	teaspoon vanilla extract

IN A SMALL SKILLET, sauté pecans in butter until lightly browned, 3 to 5 minutes. Set aside to cool. In a medium saucepan, combine brown sugar, beaten eggs, and half-and-half. Stir over low heat until mixture simmers. Stirring occasionally, simmer gently 2 minutes; set aside. Stir in whipping cream, vanilla, and toasted pecans. Pour into ice cream canister. Freeze in ice cream maker according to manufacturer's directions; or follow refrigerator-freezer instructions on page 11.

1 serving contains:

Cal	Carb	Fat	Chol	Calcium
373	40g	22g	126mg	119mg

Pecan-Chocolate Crunch Ice Cream

ENJOY THE FLAVOR OF A CHILLED NEW ORLEANS PRALINE WITH MELTED CHOCOLATE INSIDE.

| Makes about 2 quarts |

- 1 cup butter or margarine
- 1 (6-ounce) package semisweet chocolate pieces (1 cup)
- 1 (12-ounce) can evaporated milk
- 1 cup packed brown sugar
- 4 egg yolks, beaten
- 1 teaspoon vanilla extract
- ½ cup chopped pecans
- ½ cup flaked coconut
- 2 cups half-and-half

IN A MEDIUM SAUCEPAN, combine butter or margarine, chocolate pieces, evaporated milk, brown sugar, and beaten egg yolks. Cook and stir over low heat until chocolate and sugar dissolve and mixture thickens slightly. Beat with a whisk until smooth. Cool about 10 minutes. Stir in vanilla, pecans, coconut, and half-and-half. Pour into ice cream canister. Freeze in ice cream maker according to manufacturer's directions; or follow refrigerator-freezer instructions on page 11.

1 serving contains:

Cal	Carb	Fat	Chol	Calcium
422	32g	32g	130mg	170mg

Pecan-Butterscotch Ripple Ice Cream

TURN PLAIN VANILLA INTO AN ELEGANT TREAT. LET THE ICE CREAM SOFTEN ENOUGH TO SWIRL SAUCE THROUGH. DON'T LET IT MELT.

| Makes about 2 quarts |

- ½ cup lightly packed brown sugar
- 2 tablespoons light corn syrup
- ¼ cup milk
- 1 tablespoon butter or margarine
- ¼ cup finely chopped pecans
- ¼ teaspoon vanilla extract
- ½ gallon vanilla ice cream, slightly softened

PLACE A 9-INCH-SQUARE PAN in freezer to chill. In a small saucepan, combine brown sugar, corn syrup, and milk. Cook and stir over medium heat until slightly thickened, 7 or 8 minutes. Stir in butter or margarine, pecans, and vanilla. Cool to room temperature. Spoon softened ice cream into chilled pan. Pour cooled sauce in ribbons across top of ice cream. Pull a metal spatula or table knife back and forth evenly through ice cream to give a marbled effect. Cover with plastic wrap or foil. Place in freezer; freeze at least one hour or until firm, 3 to 6 hours.

1 serving contains:

Cal	Carb	Fat	Chol	Calcium
249	33g	12g	42mg	128mg

Maple-Pecan Frozen Yogurt

STORES WELL IN REFRIGERATOR-FREEZER WITHOUT LOSING ITS SMOOTH, RICH TEXTURE.

Makes about 1 quart

- ½ cup chopped pecans
- ¾ cup low-fat milk
- 1 egg, slightly beaten
- 1 cup maple-flavored syrup
- ½ teaspoon vanilla extract
- 1 cup plain low-fat yogurt, stirred

PLACE PECANS in pie pan. Heat in 350F (177C) oven about 10 minutes or until lightly toasted; set aside to cool. In medium saucepan, combine milk, beaten egg, and maple-flavored syrup. Cook and stir over medium-low heat until slightly thickened. Remove from heat; cool. Add vanilla, toasted pecans, and yogurt. Freeze in ice cream maker according to manufacturer's directions; or follow refrigerator-freezer instructions on page 11.

1 serving contains:

Cal	Carb	Fat	Chol	Calcium
258	42g	9g	39mg	156mg

Coconut-Macadamia Ice Cream

TWO FAVORITE NUTS ARE COMBINED TO MAKE THIS A DOUBLE DELIGHT.

Makes about 1 quart

¾	cup chopped macadamia nuts
1	tablespoon butter or margarine
2	eggs, beaten
¾	cup sugar
1½	cups half-and-half
½	cup whipping cream
1	cup flaked coconut
1	teaspoon vanilla extract

IN A SMALL SKILLET, sauté nuts in butter or margarine until lightly browned, 3 to 5 minutes. Set aside to cool. In a medium saucepan, combine beaten eggs, sugar, and half-and-half. Cook and stir over low heat until thickened. Remove from heat; stir in nuts, whipping cream, coconut, and vanilla. Pour into ice cream canister. Freeze in ice cream maker according to manufacturer's directions; or follow refrigerator-freezer instructions on page 11.

1 serving contains:

Cal	Carb	Fat	Chol	Calcium
376	36g	25g	98mg	80mg

White Chocolate-Macadamia Frozen Yogurt

YOU CAN SUBSTITUTE A WHITE-CHOCOLATE-WITH-ALMONDS CANDY BAR AND OMIT THE MACADAMIAS.

Makes about 1 quart

- 1 cup low-fat milk
- ¼ cup sugar
- 2 tablespoons light corn syrup
- 1 (8-ounce) carton egg substitute (such as Egg Beaters®), thawed
- 4 ounces white baking bar or white chocolate candy bar, finely chopped
- ¼ cup macadamia nuts, coarsely chopped*
- ½ teaspoon vanilla extract
- 1 cup plain low-fat yogurt, stirred

IN A 2-QUART SAUCEPAN, combine milk, sugar, corn syrup, and egg substitute. Stir until well blended. Cook and stir over moderate heat until mixture is very thick. Remove from heat; immediately stir in chopped white chocolate. Add macadamia nuts and vanilla; cool. Stir in yogurt. Freeze in ice cream maker according to manufacturer's directions; or follow refrigerator-freezer instructions on page 11.

If this recipe will be frozen in a refrigerator-freezer, see instructions before adding this ingredient.

1 serving contains:

Cal	Carb	Fat	Chol	Calcium
265	30g	12g	9mg	187mg

Hazelnut Gelato

ITALY IS RENOWNED FOR ITS SUPERB ICE CREAM. THIS RECIPE RECREATES ONE OF THE COUNTRY'S MOST FAMOUS FLAVORS.

Makes about 2 quarts

- 2 **cups hazelnuts, roasted and rubbed**
- 3 **cups milk**
- 1 **cup sugar**
- 4 **egg yolks**
- 2 **cups whipping cream**
- ½ **teaspoon vanilla extract**

IN BLENDER OR FOOD PROCESSOR, blend nuts until pieces resemble fine breadcrumbs. In a saucepan, combine nuts, milk, and sugar. Stir over heat until sugar dissolves and mixture comes to a boil; set aside. Cover and cool. Line a strainer with cheesecloth. Strain cooled milk mixture. In a bowl, beat egg yolks until thick and lemon colored, about 5 minutes. In a saucepan, combine egg yolks and milk mixture. Cook over low heat until mixture coats a spoon. Cool. Stir in whipping cream and vanilla. Pour into ice cream canister. Freeze in ice cream maker according to manufacturer's directions; or follow refrigerator-freezer instructions on page 11.

1 serving contains:

Cal	Carb	Fat	Chol	Calcium
380	24g	30g	134mg	142mg

Alpine Peanut Ice Cream

IMAGINE MILK-CHOCOLATE CHIP WITH PIECES OF PEANUTS ADDED TO VANILLA ICE CREAM.

Makes about 1 quart

1	(5-inch) vanilla bean, cut into ¼-inch pieces
½	cup sugar
2	teaspoons cornstarch
2½	cups half-and-half
2	tablespoons light corn syrup
1	egg, beaten
½	cup whipping cream
¾	cup chocolate-covered peanuts, coarsely chopped

PURÉE VANILLA BEAN AND SUGAR in blender or food processor fitted with a metal blade until only small specks of bean are visible. In medium saucepan, combine sugar mixture with cornstarch. Stir in half-and-half and corn syrup. Cook and stir over medium-high heat until mixture boils; cook and stir 1 minute longer. Remove from heat. Stir 1 cup hot mixture into beaten egg. Stirring constantly, pour egg mixture into remaining hot mixture. Cook and stir over low heat 2 or 3 minutes until thickened. Strain to remove vanilla bean. Stir in whipping cream and chocolate-covered peanuts. Pour into ice cream canister. Freeze in ice cream maker according to manufacturer's directions; or follow refrigerator-freezer instructions on page 11.

1 serving contains:

Cal	Carb	Fat	Chol	Calcium
396	37g	26g	101mg	143mg

Walnut-Maple Ice Cream

BE SURE TO USE GENUINE MAPLE SYRUP WHEN MAKING THIS CREAMY NEW ENGLAND TREAT.

Makes about 1 quart

- ½ cup walnuts
- 2 egg yolks, beaten
- 1 cup maple syrup
- ¾ cup milk
- ½ teaspoon vanilla extract
- 1 cup half-and-half or whipping cream

PREHEAT OVEN to 325F (165C). Arrange walnuts over bottom of a shallow 12" x 7" baking pan. Toast in preheated oven until golden brown, 5 to 7 minutes. In blender or food processor fitted with a metal blade, process toasted nuts until finely chopped; set aside. In a medium saucepan, combine beaten egg yolks, maple syrup, and milk. Cook and stir over low heat until slightly thickened. Stir in chopped nuts, vanilla, and half-and-half or whipping cream. Cool to room temperature. Pour into ice cream canister. Freeze in ice cream maker according to manufacturer's directions; or follow refrigerator-freezer instructions on page 11.

1 serving contains:

Cal	Carb	Fat	Chol	Calcium
295	40g	13g	90mg	128mg

Snickers® Candy Ice Cream

THIS POPULAR CANDY TURNS INTO A SENSATIONAL FROZEN TREAT.

Makes about 1 quart

- ⅓ cup brown sugar
- 2 teaspoons cornstarch
- 1 (12-ounce) can low-fat evaporated milk
- 2 (2.07-ounce) Snickers® candy bars, chilled and cut into ¼-inch pieces
- 1 cup half-and-half

IN A MEDIUM SAUCEPAN, combine brown sugar and cornstarch. Add evaporated milk. Cook and stir over medium heat until bubbly and thickened. Cook 1 minute longer. Remove from heat; stir in half of candy. Add half-and-half; cool. Stir in remaining candy. Pour into ice cream canister. Freeze in ice cream maker according to manufacturer's directions; or follow refrigerator-freezer instructions on page 11.

1 serving contains:

Cal	Carb	Fat	Chol	Calcium
243	33g	9g	20mg	256mg

Toffee-Coffee Ice Cream

BREAK THE WRAPPED CANDY BARS INTO SMALL PIECES BY STRIKING WITH THE HANDLE OF A KNIFE.

Makes about 2 quarts

- 3 eggs, beaten
- ⅔ cup sugar
- 3 cups milk
- 2 tablespoons instant-coffee crystals
- 3 (1⅙-ounce) Heath® candy bars, chilled
- ½ teaspoon vanilla extract
- 2 cups whipping cream

IN A MEDIUM SAUCEPAN, combine beaten eggs, sugar, milk, and coffee crystals. Cook and stir over low heat until sugar and coffee crystals dissolve and mixture thickens slightly. Cool to room temperature. Break chilled candy in wrappers into small pieces by striking sharply with handle of a knife. Stir broken candy, vanilla, and whipping cream into cooled mixture. Pour into ice cream canister. Freeze in ice cream maker according to manufacturer's directions; or follow refrigerator-freezer instructions on page 11.

1 serving contains:

Cal	Carb	Fat	Chol	Calcium
260	18g	19g	117mg	116mg

Licorice-Stick Ice Cream

CHOOSE YOUR FAVORITE—RED OR BLACK LICORICE.

Makes about 1 quart

2 egg yolks

½ cup sugar

1 cup whipping cream

1 cup milk

1 cup licorice, cut in ¼-inch pieces (about 2½ ounces)

½ cup milk

IN A SMALL BOWL, beat egg yolks until thick and lemon colored, 4 or 5 minutes. In a heavy medium saucepan, combine beaten egg yolks, sugar, whipping cream, and 1 cup milk. Cook and stir over low heat until mixture thickens slightly and coats a spoon; set aside. In blender or food processor fitted with a metal blade, combine cut-up licorice pieces and ½ cup milk. Process until licorice pieces resemble grains of cooked rice. Stir into egg mixture. Cool to room temperature. Pour into ice cream canister. Freeze in ice cream maker according to manufacturer's directions; or follow refrigerator-freezer instructions on page 11.

1 serving contains:

Cal	Carb	Fat	Chol	Calcium
309	31g	20g	134mg	106mg

Peppermint-Stick Ice Cream

STIR MORE CRUSHED CANDY INTO THE FINISHED ICE CREAM TO GET A STRONGER PEPPERMINT FLAVOR.

Makes about 1 quart

- 2 egg yolks, beaten
- ½ cup sugar
- 1 cup milk
- 1 cup half-and-half or whipping cream
- ½ cup crushed peppermint-stick candy

IN A SMALL SAUCEPAN, combine beaten egg yolks, sugar, and milk. Cook and stir over low heat until mixture is slightly thickened and coats a spoon. Remove from heat. Stir in half-and-half or whipping cream and ¼ cup crushed candy. Cool to room temperature. Pour into ice cream canister. Freeze in ice cream maker according to manufacturer's directions; or follow refrigerator-freezer instructions on page 11. When frozen, stir in remaining crushed candy.

1 serving contains:

Cal	Carb	Fat	Chol	Calcium
236	39g	8g	91mg	99mg

Peppermint Frozen Yogurt

SPRINKLE EXTRA CRUSHED PEPPERMINT OVER EACH SERVING FOR A FESTIVE PRESENTATION.

Makes about 1 quart

- 1 cup low-fat milk
- 1 teaspoon unflavored gelatin
- ½ cup sugar
- ½ cup crushed peppermint-stick candy (about 2¾ ounces)*
- 1½ cups plain low-fat yogurt, stirred

IN A SMALL SAUCEPAN, combine milk and gelatin; let stand 1 minute. Stir over low heat until gelatin dissolves; add sugar. Combine with ½ of the crushed peppermint candy. Cool; stir in yogurt. Freeze in ice cream maker according to manufacturer's directions. When frozen stir in remaining crushed peppermint. Or follow refrigerator-freezer instructions on page 11. Stir in remaining peppermint after final processing or beating.

If this recipe will be frozen in a refrigerator-freezer, see page 11 before adding the remaining half of this ingredient.

1 serving contains:

Cal	Carb	Fat	Chol	Calcium
173	36g	1g	5mg	163mg

Oreo® Cookie Frozen Yogurt

IT TAKES ABOUT 8 DOUBLE COOKIES WITH FILLING TO MAKE ENOUGH CRUMBLE.

Makes about 1 quart

2	teaspoons cornstarch
½	cup sugar
1	egg, slightly beaten
1½	cups low-fat milk
1	teaspoon vanilla extract
1	cup plain low-fat yogurt, stirred
8	Oreo® cookies*, coarsely chopped (1 cup)

IN A MEDIUM SAUCEPAN, combine cornstarch and sugar. Stir in egg and milk. Cook and stir over moderate heat until mixture simmers and thickens slightly. Cook and stir about 2 minutes longer. Remove from heat; cool. Add vanilla and yogurt to cool egg mixture; then stir in ½ cup chopped cookies. Freeze in ice cream maker according to manufacturer's directions. When mixture is frozen, stir in remaining ½ cup chopped cookies. Or follow refrigerator-freezer instructions on page 11. Stir in remaining ½ cup chopped cookies after final processing or beating.

If this recipe will be frozen in a refrigerator-freezer, see page 11 before adding the remaining ½ cup chopped cookies.

1 serving contains:

Cal	Carb	Fat	Chol	Calcium
202	34g	5g	40mg	154mg

Butterfinger® Frozen Yogurt

IT'S LIGHT AND FLUFFY, WITH TINY PIECES OF BUTTERFINGER® BARS FOUND THROUGHOUT.

Makes about 1 quart

1	cup low-fat milk
1	(1.3-ounce) envelope Dream Whip® whipped topping mix
1/3	cup sugar
2	regular-size Butterfinger® bars (about 4 ounces)
1 1/2	cups plain low-fat yogurt, stirred
1/2	teaspoon vanilla extract

IN A MEDIUM BOWL, gradually add milk to topping mix; stir until well mixed. Add sugar. Quarter candy bars; coarsely crush in blender or food processor fitted with a metal blade. Stir crushed candy, yogurt, and vanilla into milk mixture. Freeze in ice cream maker according to manufacturer's directions; or follow refrigerator-freezer instructions on page 11.

1 serving contains:

Cal	Carb	Fat	Chol	Calcium
234	36g	6g	6mg	168mg

Peanut-Butter Cups Frozen Yogurt

PEANUT-BUTTER CUPS ARE AVAILABLE IN DIFFERENT SIZES. THE TWO-PEANUT-BUTTER-CUP PACKAGE WEIGHS SLIGHTLY LESS THAN 1 OUNCE PER CUP. YOU'LL NEED 16 TO 18 MINIATURE CUPS TO EQUAL 4 OUNCES.

Makes about 1 quart

2	teaspoons cornstarch
1/3	cup sugar
4	ounces milk chocolate
1/4	cup light corn syrup
1 1/4	cups low-fat milk
1/2	teaspoon vanilla extract
1	cup plain low-fat yogurt, stirred
4	ounces peanut-butter cups, chopped

IN A MEDIUM SAUCEPAN, combine cornstarch and sugar. Stir in milk chocolate, corn syrup, and milk. Cook and stir over medium heat until mixture simmers and chocolate melts. Remove from heat. Stir in vanilla and yogurt; cool. Freeze in ice cream maker according to manufacturer's directions. When frozen stir in chopped peanut-butter cups. Or follow refrigerator-freezer instructions on page 11, and stir in chopped peanut-butter cups after final processing or beating.

1 serving contains:

Cal	Carb	Fat	Chol	Calcium
332	49g	13g	10mg	189mg

Peanut-Butter-Caramel Frozen Yogurt

YOU CAN SUBSTITUTE 1 TEASPOON VANILLA EXTRACT AND 1 CUP PLAIN LOW-FAT YOGURT FOR 1 CUP VANILLA YOGURT.

Makes about 1 quart

7 ounces Kraft® caramel squares (about 25 squares)

1½ cups fat-free milk

½ cup peanut butter (creamy or chunky)

1 cup vanilla low-fat yogurt, stirred

REMOVE AND DISCARD candy caramel wrappers. In a 1-quart saucepan, combine caramels and milk. Cook over very low heat, stirring frequently, about 8 to 10 minutes or until caramels dissolve. Add peanut butter and continue cooking and stirring until mixture is well blended. Remove from heat; cool. Stir in yogurt. Freeze in ice cream maker according to manufacturer's directions; or follow refrigerator-freezer instructions on page 11.

1 serving contains:

Cal	Carb	Fat	Chol	Calcium
320	39g	14g	5mg	218mg

Grasshopper Frozen Yogurt

WITHOUT DOUBT, THIS DESSERT, SERVED AT YOUR NEXT DINNER PARTY, WILL ENHANCE YOUR REPUTATION AS A HOST OR HOSTESS.

Makes about 1 quart

1	cup low-fat milk
1	(1.3-ounce) envelope whipped topping mix
¼	cup sugar
3	tablespoons green crème de menthe liqueur
2	tablespoons white crème de cacao liqueur
1½	cups plain low-fat yogurt, stirred
6 to 8	chocolate cookies, crushed (about ½ cup coarse crumbs)

IN A MEDIUM BOWL, gradually add milk to topping mix; stir until well mixed. Add sugar, crème de menthe, and crème de cacao. Stir in yogurt. Freeze in ice cream maker according to manufacturer's directions; or follow refrigerator-freezer instructions on page 11. At serving time, sprinkle about 1 tablespoon crushed chocolate cookies over each serving.

1 serving contains:

Cal	Carb	Fat	Chol	Calcium
211	31g	4g	6mg	165mg

Crunchy Toffee Bar Frozen Yogurt

FOR A MORE PRONOUNCED TOFFEE FLAVOR AND A CRUNCHIER TEXTURE, MAKE THIS FROZEN YOGURT WITH THREE DOUBLE CANDY BARS.

Makes about 1 quart

- 1 (12-ounce) can evaporated low-fat milk
- 1 teaspoon unflavored gelatin
- 1/3 cup brown sugar
- 2 or 3 double Heath® candy bars (about 2 1/4 to 3 1/2 ounces)
- 1 cup plain low-fat yogurt, stirred

IN A SMALL SAUCEPAN, combine milk and gelatin; let stand 1 minute. Stir over low heat until gelatin dissolves. Add sugar; cool. Cut candy bars into quarters; coarsely crush in blender or food processor fitted with a metal blade. Stir crushed candy and yogurt into milk mixture. Freeze in ice cream maker according to manufacturer's directions; or follow refrigerator-freezer instructions on page 11.

1 serving contains:

Cal	Carb	Fat	Chol	Calcium
166	27g	3g	8mg	292mg

Chocolate-Mint Parfait Frozen Yogurt

CRÈME DE MENTHE WAFERS ARE SMALL RECTANGLES OF SOFT, PALE GREEN MINT CANDY SANDWICHED BETWEEN TWO LAYERS OF SMOOTH CHOCOLATE.

Makes about 1 quart

1	cup low-fat milk
1	teaspoon unflavored gelatin
½	cup sugar
1½	cups plain low-fat yogurt, stirred
18	pieces (about 3 ounces) chocolate crème de menthe candy wafers (Andes® Daydreams™ by Suchard), finely chopped
3 or 4	drops green food coloring, optional

IN A 1-QUART SAUCEPAN, combine milk and gelatin; let stand 1 minute. Add sugar; stir over low heat until gelatin dissolves; cool. Stir in yogurt and finely chopped wafers. Add food coloring, if desired. Freeze in ice cream maker according to manufacturer's directions; or follow refrigerator-freezer instructions on page 11.

1 serving contains:

Cal	Carb	Fat	Chol	Calcium
275	57g	5g	5mg	170mg

Pastel Mint Frozen Yogurt

MORE REFRESHING THAN AN AFTER-DINNER MINT.

Makes about 1 quart

1	cup low-fat milk
1	(1.3-ounce) envelope Dream Whip® whipped topping mix
⅓	cup sugar
1½	cups plain low-fat yogurt, stirred
¾	cup (about 4 ounces) pastel after-dinner mints, coarsely chopped*

IN A MEDIUM BOWL, gradually add milk to whipped topping mix; stir until well mixed. Stir in sugar and yogurt. Add coarsely chopped mints and freeze in ice cream maker according to manufacturer's directions, or follow refrigerator-freezer instructions on page 11 and add coarsely chopped mints after final processing or beating.

If this recipe will be frozen in a refrigerator-freezer, see instructions on page 11 before adding this ingredient.

1 serving contains:

Cal	Carb	Fat	Chol	Calcium
211	40g	3g	5mg	162mg

Burnt Sugar Frozen Yogurt

ALTHOUGH THE POPULAR NAME FOR THIS LIQUEFYING PROCESS IS BURNT SUGAR, THE SUGAR SHOULD BE HEATED TO A BEAUTIFUL GOLDEN COLOR, NOT DARK BROWN.

Makes about 1 quart

- ¾ cup sugar
- 1 (12-ounce) can evaporated low-fat milk
- 1 egg, slightly beaten
- 1 teaspoon vanilla extract
- 1½ cups plain low-fat yogurt, stirred

IN A HEAVY 10-INCH SKILLET, cook sugar over moderate heat until it becomes a caramel-colored liquid. Remove from heat. Gradually stir in milk. Return to low heat; stir until smooth. Stir small amount of milk mixture into beaten egg; return to skillet. Cook and stir over low heat 3 to 4 minutes until mixture thickens and coats a metal spoon. Remove from heat; cool. Stir in vanilla and yogurt. Freeze in ice cream maker according to manufacturer's directions; or follow refrigerator-freezer instructions on page 11.

1 serving contains:

Cal	Carb	Fat	Chol	Calcium
208	37g	3g	44mg	296mg

Butterscotch Frozen Yogurt

SO RICH AND SMOOTH THAT YOUR GUESTS WILL THINK IT CONTAINS WHIPPING CREAM.

Makes about 1 quart

- ⅔ cup dark brown sugar, lightly packed
- 2 teaspoons cornstarch
- ¼ cup dark corn syrup
- 1 (12-ounce) can low-fat evaporated milk
- 1 egg, slightly beaten
- ½ teaspoon vanilla extract
- 1 cup plain low-fat yogurt, stirred
- ¼ cup chopped toasted pecans, optional*

IN A MEDIUM SAUCEPAN, combine brown sugar and cornstarch. Stir in corn syrup, milk, and beaten egg. Cook and stir over medium-low heat until mixture simmers; cook and stir 2 minutes longer. Remove from heat; cool. Stir in vanilla, yogurt, and pecans, if desired. Freeze in ice cream maker according to manufacturer's directions; or follow refrigerator-freezer instructions on page 11. Stir in pecans if desired, after final processing or beating.

If this recipe will be frozen in a refrigerator-freezer, see instructions on page 11 before adding this ingredient.

1 serving contains:

Cal	Carb	Fat	Chol	Calcium
231	45h	3g	43mg	281mg

Frozen Novelties

CAKES, BONBONS, AND MORE

Chocolate-Pecan Ice Cream Bonbons

Coconut Snowballs

Double-Chocolate Ice Cream Sandwiches

Ice Cream Birthday Cake

Ice Cream Party Clown

Frozen Yogurt S'mores

POPS

Strawberry Pops

Pineapple Pops

Purple Cow Pops

Plum Frozen-Yogurt Pops

Watermelon Frozen-Yogurt Pops

Cantaloupe-Orange Pops

CUPS

Orange Frozen-Yogurt Cups

Peach Frozen-Yogurt Cups

Chocolate-Pecan
Ice Cream Bonbons

STRAWBERRY ICE CREAM ALSO MAKES A WONDERFUL FILLING FOR THIS SPECIAL TREAT.

| Makes 30 to 35 bonbons |

- 1 pint butter-pecan ice cream
- ¼ cup butter or margarine
- 1 (16-ounce) package semisweet chocolate pieces
- 3 tablespoons evaporated milk

LINE A LARGE BAKING SHEET with foil or waxed paper. Place in freezer 10 minutes. Working quickly, use large melon-baller tool to scoop balls of ice cream. Arrange ice cream balls on chilled baking sheet. Freeze 2 hours or until very firm. In a saucepan, combine butter or margarine and chocolate pieces. Stir over low heat until melted. Stir in evaporated milk. Cool. Working quickly, use a fork to lift frozen balls of ice cream one at a time to dip into cooled chocolate mixture. Quickly turn with fork to coat evenly. Lift from sauce and arrange on baking sheet. Repeat dipping until all bonbons have been coated. Freeze until serving time.

1 bonbon contains:

Cal	Carb	Fat	Chol	Calcium
81	8g	6g	19mg	21mg

Coconut Snowballs

TO CELEBRATE A BIRTHDAY, INSERT ONE SMALL CANDLE IN TOP OF EACH SNOWBALL.

Makes 8 servings

- 1 quart vanilla or cherry ice cream
- 1 cup flaked coconut
- 8 mint sprigs
- 4 candied cherries, halved

Chocolate sauce, if desired

PLACE A BAKING SHEET IN FREEZER to chill, at least 10 minutes. Using a large ice cream scoop, make 8 large ice cream balls. Arrange on chilled baking sheet. Immediately place baking sheet with ice cream balls in freezer. Freeze at least 1 hour or until firm. Spread coconut in a pie pan or on a large sheet of foil. Roll firmly frozen ice cream balls in coconut until evenly coated. Return to freezer; freeze until firm, 1 to 3 hours. To serve, top each snowball with a sprig of mint and a half cherry. Serve plain or with chocolate sauce, if desired.

1 serving contains:

Cal	Carb	Fat	Chol	Calcium
197	18g	14g	29mg	87mg

Double-Chocolate Ice Cream Sandwiches

LET YOUR CHILDREN HELP MAKE THESE FOR THEIR NEXT GATHERING OF FRIENDS.

Makes 32 sandwiches

- 64 individual graham crackers (about 1 pound)
- ¾ cup peanut butter
- ¾ cup thick fudge ice cream topping
- ½ gallon chocolate ice cream in rectangular carton

SPREAD ONE SIDE of 32 graham crackers with peanut butter; set aside. Spread one side of remaining graham crackers with fudge topping. Remove carton from ice cream and discard. Place ice cream broadside down on a cutting board. Cut crosswise into eight ¾-inch slices. Cut each slide in fourths. Sandwich one piece of ice cream between a fudge-coated and a peanut butter-coated cracker. Place each sandwich in a small plastic bag or wrap each in foil. Freeze until firm, 1 to 3 hours.

1 sandwich contains:

Cal	Carb	Fat	Chol	Calcium
194	26g	9g	11mg	48mg

Ice Cream Birthday Cake

TRULY A CAKE TO BE REMEMBERED. SUBSTITUTE YOUR FAVORITE ICE CREAM AND SHERBET FLAVORS FOR THE ONES WE USED.

Makes 12 to 16 servings

- 1 quart chocolate ice cream, slightly softened
- 1 quart orange sherbet, slightly softened
- 1 quart vanilla ice cream, softened
- 1 cup whipping cream
- 1 tablespoon powdered sugar
- 2 tablespoons unsweetened cocoa powder

PLACE TWO 8-INCH-ROUND CAKE PANS in freezer for 10 minutes. Spread chocolate ice cream in one chilled cake pan and orange sherbet in the other. Cover with foil or plastic wrap and freeze until firm. Place a serving plate in freezer to chill. Spoon vanilla ice cream into a bowl and set aside. Working rapidly, remove cover and run tip of spatula around edge of frozen chocolate ice cream. Wipe pan with warm damp cloth. Invert onto chilled plate. Spread ¼-inch softened vanilla ice cream over top of chocolate layer; set aside. Remove cover of frozen orange sherbet. Invert onto top of vanilla layer. Spread ¼-inch softened vanilla ice cream over orange layer. Spread remaining vanilla ice cream over sides of cake. Freeze at least 1 hour or until firm. In a bowl, whip cream and gradually beat in powdered sugar and cocoa powder until stiff. Spoon into a pastry bag; decorate cake. Return to freezer at least 15 minutes before serving.

1 serving contains:

Cal	Carb	Fat	Chol	Calcium
347	45g	18g	65mg	154mg

Ice Cream Party Clown

**HAVE A CIRCUS THEME FOR YOUR CHILD'S NEXT BIRTHDAY PARTY.
MAKE ONE CLOWN FOR EACH GUEST.**

Makes 8 servings

- 1 quart vanilla or chocolate ice cream
- 8 raisins, cut in half
- 4 long red gumdrops, cut in half lengthwise
- 1/3 cup toasted coconuts
- 2 tablespoons butter or margarine, melted
- 1 tablespoon unsweetened cocoa powder

- 1 1/2 tablespoons milk
- 1 cup sifted powdered sugar
- 8 ice cream cones
- 2 tablespoons multicolored candy cake decorations
- 8 (3-inch) chocolate-chip cookies, oatmeal cookies, or sugar cookies

CHILL A BAKING SHEET IN FREEZER, at least 10 minutes. Using a large scoop, make 8 ice cream balls for clown heads. Place on chilled baking sheet. Working quickly, place 2 raisin halves on each ball for eyes; a piece of gumdrop for the mouth. Sprinkle coconut on top of each for hair. Immediately place baking sheet in freezer. Freeze until firm, about 3 hours. In a bowl, combine butter or margarine, cocoa powder, milk, and powdered sugar; beat until smooth. Spread a thin layer of frosting on outside of each cone; sprinkle with cake decorations. Refrigerate until frosting sets. To serve, place one cookie in center of each plate; top with a frozen clown's head; place a frosted cone, upside down, on each head. Serve immediately.

1 serving contains:

Cal	Carb	Fat	Chol	Calcium
398	53g	20g	44mg	102mg

Frozen Yogurt S'Mores

WE'RE NEVER TOO OLD TO ENJOY THIS CHILDHOOD TREAT.

Makes 4 servings

- ½ cup crushed graham crackers (about 6 squares)
- 1 tablespoon melted margarine or butter
- 1 cup chocolate frozen yogurt, page 37, slightly softened
- ¼ cup marshmallow cream, stirred
- ½ teaspoon lukewarm water

IN A SMALL BOWL, combine graham cracker crumbs and margarine or butter. Line 4 custard cups with paper baking liners. Press about half of crumb mixture on bottom of liners; chill. Working quickly, lightly press half of frozen chocolate yogurt over chilled graham cracker mixture. Stir marshmallow cream with lukewarm water until smooth; spoon over yogurt in each cup. Then top with remaining frozen yogurt. Sprinkle with remaining crumb mixture. Freeze in refrigerator-freezer at least 2 hours or until firm.

1 serving contains:

Cal	Carb	Fat	Chol	Calcium
235	40g	6g	20mg	78mg

Strawberry Pops

POPULAR SNACK ON HOT AFTERNOONS.

Makes 5 (5-ounce) or 8 (3-ounce) ice pops

1 (10-ounce) package frozen
strawberries, thawed

1 cup water

½ (6.2-ounce) envelope
sweetened strawberry-
flavored drink mix (½ cup)

IN A BLENDER OR FOOD PROCESSOR fitted with a metal blade, purée strawberries. Add water and drink mix. Process 3 to 5 seconds or until blended. Pour into 8 (3-ounce) or 5 (5-ounce) paper cups. Cover with foil or plastic wrap. Freeze until slushy, about 1 hour. Insert ice-pop stick in center of each cup; freeze until firm, 1 to 3 hours. To serve, peel off paper.

**1 pop with sugar-sweetened
drink mix contains:**

Cal	Carb	Fat	Chol	Calcium
25	6g	0g	0mg	5mg

**1 pop with Nutra Sweet® sweetened
drink mix contains:**

Cal	Carb	Fat	Chol	Calcium
13	3g	0g	0mg	5mg

Pineapple Pops

ICY-SWEET PINEAPPLE IS A SATISFYING SNACK ON A WARM SUMMER DAY.

Makes 5 (3-ounce), 3 (5-ounce) or 7 (2-ounce) ice pops

- 1 (8-ounce) can crushed pineapple in juice
- 1 teaspoon unflavored gelatin
- 1 tablespoon honey
- 1 large banana, peeled, mashed

IN A SMALL SAUCEPAN, combine pineapple and gelatin; let stand 1 minute. Add honey; cook and stir over low heat until gelatin dissolves. Stir in mashed banana. Pour into 5 (3-ounce) or 3 (5-ounce) paper cups or 7 (2-ounce) popsicle molds. Place in freezer until partially frozen. Insert an ice-pop stick in center of each cup or mold. Freeze until firm. To serve, peel off paper cups or dip molds in lukewarm water and remove pops.

1 pop contains:

Cal	Carb	Fat	Chol	Calcium
67	17g	0g	0mg	8mg

Purple Cow Pops

SO QUICK, SO EASY, SO PURPLE!

Makes 6 (3-ounce) or 8 (2-ounce) pops

- ¾ cup Concord grape juice
- ¼ cup light corn syrup
- ¾ cup plain low-fat yogurt, stirred

IN A MEDIUM BOWL, combine grape juice and corn syrup. Stir in yogurt. Pour into 6 or 8 plastic popsicle molds or paper cups (2- or 3-ounce). Place in refrigerator-freezer until partially frozen. Insert an ice-pop stick in each cup or mold. Freeze until firm. To serve, peel off paper cups or dip plastic mold in lukewarm water very briefly and remove frozen-yogurt pops from mold.

1 pop contains:

Cal	Carb	Fat	Chol	Calcium
74	17g	1g	2mg	58mg

Plum Frozen-Yogurt Pops

FOR A CHANGE OF PACE, TRY THIS NUTRITIOUS SNACK.

Makes 8 (3-ounce) or 12 (2-ounce) pops

- ½ cup orange juice
- 1 teaspoon unflavored gelatin
- 4 fresh plums, seeded and quartered
- 3 tablespoons sugar
- 2 tablespoons honey
- 1 cup low-fat vanilla yogurt, stirred

IN A SMALL SAUCEPAN, combine orange juice and gelatin; let stand 1 minute. Cook and stir over low heat until gelatin dissolves. Remove from heat; set aside. In blender or food processor fitted with a metal blade, combine plums, sugar, and honey. Process until plums are finely chopped. In a bowl, combine plum mixture, dissolved gelatin and yogurt. Spoon into 8 (3-ounce) paper cups or 12 (2-ounce) popsicle molds. Place in refrigerator-freezer until partially frozen. Insert an ice-pop stick in each cup or mold. Freeze until firm. To serve, peel off paper cups or dip plastic mold in lukewarm water very briefly and remove frozen-yogurt pickups from mold.

1 pop contains:

Cal	Carb	Fat	Chol	Calcium
87	19g	1g	2mg	56mg

Watermelon Frozen-Yogurt Pops

A SOPHISTICATED COMBINATION OF FLAVORS THAT APPEALS TO ADULTS AND CHILDREN.

Makes 9 pops

- ½ cup fresh or frozen unsweetened raspberries
- 2 cups watermelon cubes, seeded
- ½ cup sugar
- ⅛ teaspoon almond extract
- 1 cup plain low-fat or fat-free yogurt, stirred

IN A BLENDER OR FOOD PROCESSOR fitted with a metal blade, purée raspberries. Strain; discard seeds. Purée watermelon with sugar. In medium bowl, combine strained raspberries, puréed watermelon, almond extract, and yogurt. Pour into 9 (3-ounce) paper cups. Place in refrigerator freezer. When partially frozen, or after about 1 hour, insert an ice-pop stick in center of each pop. Freeze until firm. To serve, remove paper cups.

1 pop contains:

Cal	Carb	Fat	Chol	Calcium
75	16g	1g	2mg	54mg

Cantaloupe-Orange Pops

HERE IS A TRULY HEALTHFUL FROSTY SNACK.

Makes 7 (3-ounce), 4 (5-ounce), or 10 (2-ounce) pops

- ½ cup orange juce
- 1 teaspoon unflavored gelatin
- 2 cups cubed cantaloupe
- 2 teaspoons honey
- ½ cup low-fat milk
- ⅛ teaspoon ground ginger

IN A SMALL SAUCEPAN, combine orange juice and gelatin; let stand 1 minute. Cook and stir over low heat until gelatin dissolves. In blender or food processor fitted with metal blade, purée cantaloupe with honey, milk, and ginger. Spoon into 7 (3-ounce) or 4 (5-ounce) paper cups, or 10 (2-ounce) ice-pop molds. Place in freezer until partially frozen. Insert an ice-pop stick in center of each cup or mold. Freeze until firm. To serve, peel off paper cups or dip molds in lukewarm water and remove pops.

1 pop contains:

Cal	Carb	Fat	Chol	Calcium
41	8g	0g	1mg	26mg

Orange Frozen-Yogurt Cups

WHEN FROZEN, CAREFULLY PEEL OFF PAPER CUPS OR QUICKLY DIP PLASTIC MOLDS INTO LUKEWARM WATER AND PULL FROZEN MIXTURE OUT OF INDIVIDUAL MOLD.

Makes 10 (3-ounce) or 15 (2-ounce) cups

- 1 (3-ounce) package orange-flavored gelatin
- 1 cup boiling water
- 1 cup orange juice
- 1 banana, peeled and mashed
- 1 cup plain low-fat yogurt, stirred

IN A SMALL BOWL, dissolve gelatin in boiling water. Stir in orange juice, banana, and yogurt. Spoon into 15 (2-ounce) paper cups or 10 (3-ounce) ice-pop molds. Place in refrigerator freezer until partially frozen. Insert stick in each cup or mold. Freeze until firm. To serve, peel off paper cups or dip plastic mold in lukewarm water very briefly and remove frozen yogurt from mold.

1 pop contains:

Cal	Carb	Fat	Chol	Calcium
68	15g	0g	1mg	48mg

Peach Frozen-Yogurt Cups

KEEP SEVERAL OF THESE IN THE FREEZER FOR UNEXPECTED YOUNG VISITORS.

Makes 6 (3-ounce) or 8 (2-ounce) servings

- 1 cup miniature marshmallows
- ¼ cup low-fat milk
- 1 ripe peach, peeled and quartered
- ¼ cup fresh or frozen unsweetened raspberries or strawberries
- 1 cup low-fat peach yogurt, stirred

IN A SMALL SAUCEPAN, melt marshmallows in milk over low heat; set aside to cool. In blender or food processor fitted with a metal blade, finely chop peach and berries. Add to cool marshmallow mixture and stir in yogurt. Spoon into 6 (3-ounce) paper cups or 8 (2-ounce) plastic ice-pop molds. Place in refrigerator freezer until partially frozen. Insert ice-pop stick in each cup or mold. Freeze until firm. To serve, peel off paper cups or dip plastic mold in lukewarm water very briefly and remove frozen yogurt from mold.

1 serving contains:

Cal	Carb	Fat	Chol	Calcium
74	15g	1g	3mg	83mg

Frozen Pies, Cakes, and Molds

CHOCOLATE

Chocolate-Mint Ice Cream Pie

Chocolate Ice Cream Roll

Baked Ice Cream Brownies

Baked Alaska

Chocolate Frozen-Yogurt Cheese Pie

MOCHA

Mocha Ice Cream Cheesecake

Acapulco Mocha Ice Cream Pie

OTHER FLAVORS

Eggnog-Pumpkin Ice Cream Pie

Apricot Frozen-Yogurt Cheesecake

Lime Ice Cream Cheesecake

Gingerbread Ice Cream Roll

Frozen Burnt-Almond Mousse

Peach-Vanilla Bombe

Fried Ice Cream

Frozen Yogurt-Raspberry Trifle

Chocolate-Mint Truffle Mold

Chocolate-Mint Ice Cream Pie

FREEZE THE PEPPERMINT-CREAM FILLING UNTIL IT'S FIRM ENOUGH TO CUT, BUT NOT ICY-HARD.

Makes 6 servings

- 2 egg whites
- $\frac{1}{3}$ cup granulated sugar
- $\frac{1}{4}$ teaspoon vanilla extract
- $\frac{1}{3}$ cup finely crushed chocolate-cookie crumbs
- $\frac{1}{4}$ cup chopped walnuts
- 1 cup whipping cream
- 2 tablespoons powdered sugar
- $\frac{1}{3}$ cup crushed peppermint candy
- 1 (1-ounce) square semisweet chocolate, grated

THOROUGHLY GREASE BOTTOM AND SIDE of a 9-inch pie pan; set aside. Preheat oven to 325F (165C). In a bowl, beat egg whites until soft peaks form. Gradually beat in granulated sugar until stiff glossy peaks form. Fold in vanilla, cookie crumbs, and walnuts. Spread over bottom and up sides of prepared pan. Bake 25 to 30 minutes. Cool. About 3 hours before serving, whip cream until soft peaks form. Fold in powdered sugar and peppermint candy. Spread over meringue. Sprinkle with grated chocolate. Freeze until firm, about 3 hours.

1 serving contains:

Cal	Carb	Fat	Chol	Calcium
309	31g	20g	54mg	34mg

Chocolate Ice Cream Roll

IN THE SUMMER, FILL THE ROLL WITH FRESH PEACH OR FRESH STRAWBERRY ICE CREAM.

Makes about 10 slices

4	egg whites, room temperature
$1/4$	teaspoon cream of tartar
$1/3$	cup granulated sugar
4	egg yolks
$1/3$	cup granulated sugar
1	teaspoon lemon juice
2	tablespoons water
$1/2$	cup all-purpose flour
	Powdered sugar
1	quart chocolate ice cream or Rocky Road Ice Cream, page 31

PREHEAT OVEN to 350F (175C). Grease a $15^1/_2$" x $10^1/_2$" x 1" baking pan. Line with waxed paper. Grease waxed paper; set aside. In a bowl, beat egg whites and cream of tartar until soft peaks form. Gradually beat in $1/3$ cup granulated sugar until peaks are stiff but not dry. In a medium bowl, beat egg yolks until thick and lemon colored. Gradually beat in $1/3$ cup granulated sugar, lemon juice, and water. Fold egg-yolk mixture into beaten egg whites, then fold in flour. Spread in baking pan. Bake 15 minutes. Dust a towel with powdered sugar. When cake is baked, immediately turn out onto sugared towel. Remove waxed paper. Carefully roll warm cake and towel with narrow end of cake. When cool, unroll, and remove towel. Spread with ice cream. Re-roll and wrap in foil. Freeze at least 6 hours, until very firm. To serve, cut in slices.

1 serving contains:

Cal	Carb	Fat	Chol	Calcium
223	34g	8g	103mg	69mg

Baked Ice Cream Brownies

WHEN TIME IS SHORT, BUY BROWNIES AT THE BAKERY OR USE A MIX.

Makes 9 servings

¼ cup butter or margarine	½ cup all-purpose flour
2 (1-ounce) squares unsweetened chocolate	½ cup chopped walnuts
2 eggs	9 scoops vanilla, banana, or peppermint ice cream
1 cup sugar	4 egg whites
¼ teaspoon salt	¼ teaspoon cream of tartar
½ teaspoon vanilla extract	½ cup sugar

IN A SAUCEPAN, combine butter or margarine and chocolate. Stir over low heat until melted; set aside. Preheat oven to 350F (175C). In a bowl, beat eggs until light and foamy. Beat in 1 cup sugar, salt, and vanilla. Stir in chocolate mixture, then stir in flour. Fold in walnuts. Pour into an ungreased 8-inch-square pan. Bake until mixture is set, about 20 minutes. Cool. Cut into 9 squares. Arrange on a large baking sheet. Top each brownie with a scoop of ice cream. Freeze until ice cream is very firm, 2 to 4 hours. At serving time, preheat oven to 450F (230C). Beat egg whites with cream of tartar until foamy. Gradually beat in ½ cup sugar until stiff and glossy. Quickly spoon meringue over ice cream and brownies, covering completely. Bake until lightly browned, 3 to 4 minutes. Serve immediately.

1 serving contains:

Cal	Carb	Fat	Chol	Calcium
429	58g	20g	90mg	101mg

Baked Alaska

FOR AN EXTRA-RICH BASE, USE A BROWNIE COOKIE BASE.

Makes 8 servings

- 1 quart chocolate, vanilla, or strawberry ice cream, slightly softened
- 1 (9-inch) single-layer chocolate or white cake
- 4 egg whites, room temperature
- $\frac{1}{2}$ teaspoon cream of tartar
- $\frac{1}{2}$ cup sugar

Chocolate sauce or raspberry topping

SPREAD ICE CREAM in an 8-inch-round cake pan. Cover with foil or plastic wrap. Freeze at least 2 hours or until firm. Place cake layer on a large baking sheet; refrigerate cake until ice cream is firm. Unmold ice cream by quickly dipping pan in warm water. Invert onto chilled cake. Cake will extend about $\frac{1}{2}$-inch beyond edge of ice cream. Freeze cake and ice cream about $\frac{1}{2}$ hour or until ice cream is firm. At serving time, preheat oven to 450F (230C). In a large bowl, beat egg whites and cream of tartar until soft peaks form. Gradually beat in sugar until stiff peaks form. Quickly spread meringue over cake and ice cream, covering completely. Seal meringue to baking sheet. Bake until browned, 4 to 5 minutes. Serve immediately. Cut into wedges; top with chocolate sauce or raspberry topping, if desired.

1 serving contains:

Cal	Carb	Fat	Chol	Calcium
497	79g	19g	75mg	178mg

Chocolate Frozen-Yogurt Cheese Pie

A DOUBLE CHOCOLATE DESSERT DESIGNED JUST FOR CHOCOHOLICS.

Cut into 6 or 8 wedges to serve

1	cup crushed chocolate cookies (18 to 20)
2	tablespoons melted margarine or butter
1	cup cottage cheese
¾	cup sugar
½	cup unsweetened cocoa powder
½	teaspoon vanilla extract
1	cup plain low-fat yogurt
2	egg whites

IN SMALL BOWL, combine crushed cookies and margarine or butter. Press on bottom and sides of 9-inch pie pan; chill. In blender or food processor fitted with a metal blade, combine cottage cheese, sugar, unsweetened cocoa powder, vanilla, and yogurt. Process until cottage cheese is smooth. In medium bowl, beat egg whites until stiff but not dry. Gradually fold in smooth cottage-cheese mixture. Spoon into crumb-lined pie pan. Cover with plastic wrap or foil and freeze in refrigerator-freezer for 4 hours or until firm.

1 wedge contains:

Cal	Carb	Fat	Chol	Calcium
291	46g	9g	16mg	117mg

Mocha Ice Cream Cheesecake

FOR VARIETY, SUBSTITUTE ZWIEBACK CRUMBS FOR CHOCOLATE-COOKIE CRUMBS.

Makes 8 to 10 servings

- 20 chocolate cookies, crushed (1¼ cups)
- ¼ cup butter or margarine, melted
- 2 (8-ounce) packages Neufchatel cheese, softened
- ¾ cup sugar
- 2 (1-ounce) squares semisweet chocolate, grated
- 1 tablespoon instant-coffee crystals
- 1 cup whipping cream

IN A BOWL, combine cookie crumbs and butter or margarine. Press over bottom and about 2 inches up side of an 8-inch springform pan; refrigerate. In a large bowl, beat cheese and sugar until smooth. Stir in grated chocolate and coffee; set aside. In a small bowl, whip cream until stiff. Fold whipped cream into cheese mixture. Spoon into crumb-lined pan. Cover with foil or plastic wrap. Freeze until firm, 5 to 6 hours. For easier slicing, remove from freezer and place in refrigerator 10 to 20 minutes before serving. To serve, remove side of pan.

1 serving contains:

Cal	Carb	Fat	Chol	Calcium
474	36g	35g	100mg	73mg

Acapulco Mocha Ice Cream Pie

HAVE THE FUDGE TOPPING READY AT ROOM TEMPERATURE FOR EASE IN SPREADING OVER THE PIE.

Makes 6 servings

30 chocolate cookies, crushed (1½ cups)

3 tablespoons butter, melted

1 pint coffee ice cream, slightly softened

½ cup chocolate fudge ice cream topping, room temperature

1 cup whipping cream

2 tablespoons coffee liqueur

IN A BOWL, combine cookie crumbs and cutter. Reserve ¼-cup mixture. Press remaining crumbs over bottom and up side of a 9-inch pie plate. Refrigerate about 30 minutes. Spread softened ice cream over chilled crust. Spoon fudge topping evenly over ice cream. Cover with foil or plastic wrap. Freeze until firm, about 3 hours. In a bowl, beat whipping cream until soft peaks form. Gradually beat in liqueur. Spread over top of frozen pie. Sprinkle with reserved cookie crumbs. Cut into wedges; serve immediately or return to freezer.

1 serving contains:

Cal	Carb	Fat	Chol	Calcium
615	57g	39g	151mg	160mg

Eggnog-Pumpkin Ice Cream Pie

FOR HOLIDAY ENTERTAINING, WE SUGGEST THIS PERFECT MAKE-AHEAD DESSERT.

Makes 6 servings

- 20 gingersnaps, crushed (1½ cups)
- 2 tablespoons butter or margarine, melted
- 1 pint eggnog or vanilla ice cream, softened
- 1 cup cooked pumpkin
- ¾ cup sugar
- ½ teaspoon ground cinnamon
- ¼ teaspoon ground nutmeg
- 1 tablespoon rum or brandy
- 1 cup whipping cream

Whipped cream for decoration, if desired

IN A BOWL, combine gingersnap crumbs and butter or margarine. Press over bottom and up side of a 9-inch pie pan. Refrigerate about 30 minutes. Spoon softened ice cream over chilled crust. Smooth surface with back of a spoon. Cover with foil or plastic wrap. Freeze until firm, about 3 hours. In a bowl, combine pumpkin, sugar, cinnamon, nutmeg, and rum or brandy; set aside. In a bowl, beat 1 cup whipping cream until soft peaks form. Fold into pumpkin mixture. Spread over ice cream. Freeze until firm, about 4 hours. For easier slicing, remove from freezer and place in refrigerator 10 to 20 minutes before serving. Decorate with additional whipped cream.

1 serving contains:

Cal	Carb	Fat	Chol	Calcium
494	57g	27g	114mg	161mg

Apricot Frozen-Yogurt Cheesecake

AVOID LAST-MINUTE PREPARATION WITH THIS SPECIAL MAKE-AHEAD DESSERT.

Makes 1 (8-inch) cheesecake

- 1½ cups crushed gingersnaps (about 24 cookies)
- ¼ cup melted margarine or butter
- 1 cup low-fat milk
- 1 teaspoon unflavored gelatin
- 1 (8-ounce) package Neufchatel cheese, cubed
- ¾ cup sugar
- ¼ teaspoon almond extract
- ¾ cup dried apricots, coarsely chopped
- 1 cup plain low-fat yogurt, stirred

IN A SMALL BOWL, combine crushed cookies and margarine or butter. Press on bottom and about 2 inches up sides of 8-inch springform pan; refrigerate. In small saucepan, combine milk and gelatin; let stand 1 minute. Cook and stir over low heat until gelatin dissolves; remove from heat. In blender or food processor fitted with metal blade, combine cheese, sugar, almond extract, and apricots. Process until well blended. Add dissolved gelatin; process very briefly. Stir into yogurt. Spoon into cookie-lined pan. Freeze in refrigerator-freezer until firm (about 2 hours).

1 serving contains:

Cal	Carb	Fat	Chol	Calcium
463	62g	20g	54mg	185mg

Lime Ice Cream Cheesecake

OUR RECIPE FEATURES A REFRESHING, LIGHT-AND-CREAMY LIME FILLING.

Makes about 12 servings

- 1 (6-ounce) box zwieback toast, crushed
- 2 tablespoons sugar
- ⅓ cup melted butter
- 1 (.25-ounce) envelope unflavored gelatin
- 1 cup sugar
- 1 cup low-fat milk
- 2 eggs, beaten
- ¼ cup lime juice
- ½ teaspoon grated lime peel
- 2 cups low-fat cottage cheese
- ½ dairy sour cream
- Whipped cream for decoration, if desired
- Grated lime peel for decoration, if desired

IN A BOWL combine zwieback crumbs, 2 tablespoons sugar and melted butter. Press over bottom and about 1½ inches up side of 9-inch springform pan; refrigerate. In a saucepan, combine gelatin and 1 cup sugar. Add milk and beaten eggs. Cook and stir over low heat until thickened; remove from heat. In blender or food processor fitted with a metal blade, process lime juice, lime peel, and cottage cheese until smooth. Combine lime-cottage cheese mixture and sour cream with cooled gelatin mixture. Pour into chilled crust; freeze until firm. To serve, remove side of pan. If desired, decorate top with whipped cream and grated lime peel. Cut into wedges.

1 serving contains:

Cal	Carb	Fat	Chol	Calcium
250	33g	10g	62mg	79mg

Gingerbread Ice Cream Roll

NOTHING IS MORE INVITING THAN THE AROMA OF GINGERBREAD BAKING. IT WILL REMIND YOU OF GRANDMA'S KITCHEN.

Makes about 10 slices

4	eggs
½	cup sugar
¾	cup all-purpose flour
½	teaspoon baking soda
¼	teaspoon salt
½	teaspoon ground cinnamon
¼	teaspoon ground allspice
½	teaspoon ground ginger
½	cup molasses
	Powdered sugar
1	quart lemon or orange ice cream, slightly softened

GREASE BOTTOM AND SIDE of a 15½" x 10½" x 1" baking pan. Line bottom with waxed paper. Grease waxed paper; set aside. Preheat oven to 375F (190C). In a bowl, beat eggs until thick and lemon colored. Gradually beat in sugar. Stir in flour, baking soda, salt, cinnamon, allspice, ginger, and molasses; beat until smooth. Pour into baking pan. Bake 12 to 15 minutes or until cake shrinks from sides of pan. Dust a towel with powdered sugar. When cake is baked, immediately turn out onto sugared towel. Remove waxed paper. Carefully roll warm cake and towel from narrow end of cake. When cool, unroll and remove towel. Spread ice cream over cake. Re-roll cake and wrap in foil. Serve immediately or freeze until serving time. To serve, cut in slices.

1 slice contains:

Cal	Carb	Fat	Chol	Calcium
213	45g	2g	85mg	45mg

Frozen Burnt-Almond Mousse

SERVE THIS LIGHT MAPLE DESSERT TOPPED WITH A CRUNCH OF ALMONDS.

Makes 8 servings

- 4 egg yolks, beaten
- ³/₄ cup maple syrup
- ³/₄ cup slivered almonds, chopped, toasted
- ³/₄ cup sugar
- ¹/₂ teaspoon vanilla extract
- 2 cups whipping cream
- Whipped cream for decoration
- Toasted chopped almonds for decoration

IN A SAUCEPAN, combine egg yolks and maple syrup. Cook and stir over low heat until thickened; set aside. Butter a 13" x 9" baking pan; sprinkle with toasted almonds; set aside. Put sugar in a skillet; stir until sugar melts and is golden. Immediately pour caramelized sugar over almonds. Cool to room temperature. Break into small pieces. In a large bowl, combine egg-yolk mixture, crumbled almond candy, and vanilla; set aside. Whip 2 cups cream until soft peaks form. Fold into almond mixture. Spoon into a 6¹/₂-cup mold. Cover and freeze until firm, 3 to 6 hours. Place a platter or tray in freezer to chill, about 30 minutes. To unmold, dip frozen mold quickly in and out of lukewarm water to depth of contents. Invert onto chilled plater or tray; remove mold. Decorate with whipped cream and almonds, if desired.

1 serving contains:

Cal	Carb	Fat	Chol	Calcium
459	43g	31g	188mg	103mg

Peach-Vanilla Bombe

USE FRESH, DRAINED, CANNED, OR FROZEN PEACHES.

Makes 10 to 12 servings

- 1 quart vanilla or butter-pecan ice cream, softened
- 4 ripe peaches, peeled, chopped
- ¼ cup light corn syrup
- 2 tablespoons peach brandy
- 1 cup whipping cream
- ⅛ teaspoon almond extract
- Whipped cream for decoration, if desired

PLACE AN 8-CUP BOMBE MOLD into freezer to chill, about 30 minutes. Working quickly, line sides and bottom of chilled mold with softened ice cream. Cover with foil or plastic wrap. Freeze until firm, 1 to 3 hours. In a bowl, combine peaches, corn syrup, and brandy. Cover and refrigerate. Whip 1 cup cream until soft peaks form. Stir in almond extract. Fold into peach mixture. Spoon peach mixture into center of bombe. Cover with plastic wrap or foil; freeze until firm, about 6 hours. Place a platter or tray in freezer to chill, about 30 minutes. To unmold, dip mold quickly in and out of warm water to depth of contents. Invert onto chilled platter or tray; remove mold. Decorate with additional whipped cream. To serve, slice crosswise, dipping knife in warm water before making each slice.

1 serving contains:

Cal	Carb	Fat	Chol	Calcium
235	24g	15g	56mg	85mg

Fried Ice Cream

A REAL SHOW-STOPPER! CRISP ON THE OUTSIDE AND FROZEN ON THE INSIDE.

Makes 6 servings

- 6 scoops chocolate or vanilla ice cream
- 1 cup finely crushed graham crackers or vanilla wafers
- ¼ teaspoon ground cinnamon
- 1 egg
- 1 tablespoon milk

Oil for deep-frying

Chocolate sauce, if desired

PLACE ICE CREAM BALLS in a 9-inch-square pan. Cover with foil or plastic wrap. Freeze until very firm, at least 3 hours. In a small bowl, combine crumbs and cinnamon. Quickly roll ice cream balls one at a time in crumbs; set crumbs aside. Freeze balls until very firm, 1 to 3 hours. In a bowl, beat egg and milk until blended. Quickly roll coated ice cream balls in egg mixture, then in crumbs again. Return to freezer; freeze until firm, 1 to 3 hours. Pour oil 3 inches deep in a deep-fryer or medium saucepan. Heat to 375F (190C). At this temperature a 1-inch cube of bread will turn golden brown in 45 seconds. Use a slotted spoon to lower one ice cream ball at a time into hot oil. Fry 8 to 10 seconds on each side. Serve immediately; plain or with chocolate sauce, if desired.

1 serving contains:

Cal	Carb	Fat	Chol	Calcium
271	34g	14g	58mg	84mg

Frozen Yogurt-Raspberry Trifle

AN EASY-TO-MAKE TRIFLE FEATURING BAKERY CAKE AND TWO KINDS OF FROZEN YOGURT.

Cut crosswise into 8 or 9 slices

½ cup seedless raspberry jam

1 tablespoon Chambord black-raspberry liqueur

1 (1-pound) loaf pound cake, cut into 15 crosswise slices

1 pint vanilla frozen yogurt, slightly softened

1 pint raspberry frozen yogurt, slightly softened

1 egg white

⅓ cup nonfat dry milk

⅓ cup water

2 tablespoons sugar

LINE 9" x 5" LOAF PAN with foil or waxed paper. In small bowl, combine jam and liqueur. Set aside about 1 tablespoon jam mixture for garnish. Lightly coat one side of each slice of cake with remaining jam mixture. Line bottom and sides of loaf pan with 9 slices of cake, placing uncoated side of cake against outside and bottom of pan. Carefully spread frozen vanilla yogurt over cake in bottom of pan. Place 3 slices of cake, jam-side down, on frozen vanilla yogurt. Carefully spread frozen raspberry yogurt over cake. Top with remaining slices of cake, jam-side down. If any pieces of cake are higher than the pan, trim even with top. Freeze until firm. Unmold and remove foil or waxed paper. Beat egg white, nonfat dry milk, and water until stiff but not dry. Beat in sugar. Frost top and sides of frozen loaf. Drizzle reserved 1 tablespoon jam over top. Serve immediately or refreeze.

1 slice contains:

Cal	Carb	Fat	Chol	Calcium
400	64g	13g	131mg	212mg

Chocolate-Mint Truffle Mold

AFTER ONE BITE, THIS WILL BE A FAVORITE AT YOUR HOUSE.

Makes 8 servings

- 10 whole ladyfingers, split horizontally
- 1 cup butter, room temperature
- 2 cups sifted powdered sugar
- 3 (1-ounce) squares unsweetened chocolate, melted
- 4 eggs
- ½ teaspoon peppermint extract

Whipped cream for decoration, if desired

IN BOTTOM OF AN 8-INCH SPRINGFORM PAN, arrange 10 ladyfinger halves cut side down like spokes of a wheel. Reserve remaining ladyfinger halves. In a large bowl, beat butter and powdered sugar until light and fluffy. Beat in melted chocolate. Add eggs one at a time, beating well after each addition. Stir in peppermint extract. Gently spoon into pan without disturbing ladyfingers in pan. Over top of filling, arrange reserved ladyfinger halves cut side down like spokes of a wheel. Cover pan with foil or plastic wrap. Place in freezer; freeze at least 4 hours. Remove side of pan; cut into wedges. Decorate with whipped cream, if desired.

1 bar contains:

Cal	Carb	Fat	Chol	Calcium
422	34g	32g	17mg	0mg

Soda Fountain and Bar Concoctions

SODA FOUNTAIN
Classic Banana Split
Blueberry Melba
Cherries Jubilee
Fudge Sundae
Praline Parfait
Root-Beer Sorbet

SAUCES
Almond-Apricot-Brandy Sauce
Apricot Sauce
Favorite Fudge Sauce
Gingered Suzette Sauce
Pineapple Sauce
Raspberry-Currant Sauce
Whipped Yogurt

DRINKS
Strawberry Soda
Ice Cream After-Dinner Drinks
Bellini Freeze
Frozen Kir Spritzer
Ice Cream Smoothies

Classic Banana Split

PERSONALIZE THIS BASIC COMBINATION WITH YOUR FAVORITE ICE CREAM FLAVORS AND TOPPINGS.

Makes 1 serving

- 1 banana, peeled, split in half lengthwise
- 1 scoop vanilla ice cream
- 1 scoop chocolate ice cream
- 1 scoop strawberry ice cream
- 1 tablespoon chocolate syrup
- 1 tablespoon marshmallow cream
- 1 tablespoon strawberry preserves or raspberry topping

Whipped cream

Chopped nuts

- 3 maraschino cherries

ARRANGE HALF OF BANANA on each side of shallow oval dish. Place scoops of vanilla, chocolate, and strawberry ice cream in a row between banana slices. Spoon chocolate syrup over vanilla ice cream, marshmallow over chocolate ice cream, and strawberry preserves or raspberry topping over strawberry ice cream. Top each scoop of ice cream with whipped cream, chopped nuts, and a maraschino cherry.

1 serving contains:

Cal	Carb	Fat	Chol	Calcium
766	129g	28g	81mg	255mg

Blueberry Melba

CREATE AN EYE-CATCHING DESSERT WITH THIS WINNING COMBINATION OF FRUIT AND ICE CREAM.

| Makes 6 servings |

½ cup sugar

1 tablespoon cornstarch

¾ cup port wine

2 tablespoons lemon juice

1½ cups fresh or frozen blueberries, thawed

6 fresh or canned peach halves, drained

6 scoops vanilla ice cream

IN SMALL SAUCEPAN, combine sugar and cornstarch. Stir in wine and lemon juice. Cook and stir over low heat until thickened and translucent. Stir in blueberries; simmer about 5 minutes. Cool to room temperature. To serve, arrange peach halves cut-side up in 6 sherbet glasses. Top each with 1 scoop ice cream. Spoon cooled blueberry sauce evenly over each.

1 serving contains:

Cal	Carb	Fat	Chol	Calcium
290	49g	7g	29mg	92mg

Cherries Jubilee

CONCLUDE THAT SPECIAL DINNER WITH A SPECTACULAR FLAMING DESSERT.

Makes 6 servings

1	quart vanilla ice cream
¼	cup orange liqueur
1	(16-ounce) can pitted dark sweet cherries, drained
½	cup currant jelly
1	teaspoon grated orange peel
¼	cup brandy

THREE OR FOUR HOURS before serving time, scoop 6 large ice cream balls. Place each ball in an individual serving dish and place in freezer. At same time, in a bowl, pour liqueur over cherries. Refrigerate 3 or 4 hours. At serving time, in a skillet or chafing dish, stir jelly over low heat until melted. Stir in cherries with liqueur and orange peel. Stir over low heat until mixture begins to simmer. In a small saucepan or large metal cup, heat brandy until warm, about 150F (65C). Do not let brandy become hot. Pour warmed brandy over cherry mixture. Use a match with a long stick to ignite brandy. When flame diminishes, carefully spoon cherries and sauce over each serving. Serve immediately.

1 serving contains:

Cal	Carb	Fat	Chol	Calcium
338	55g	10g	39mg	122mg

Fudge Sundae

MIX OR MATCH YOUR FAVORITE ICE CREAMS WITH HOMEMADE OR COMMERCIAL TOPPINGS.

| Makes 6 servings |

1 quart vanilla or chocolate ice cream

¾ to 1 cup Favorite Fudge Sauce (page 240)

Whipped cream

Chopped nuts

6 maraschino cherries

MAKE 6 LARGE OR 12 SMALL SCOOPS of ice cream. Divide evenly among six sherbet glasses. Spoon sauce evenly over ice cream. Top each with whipped cream, nuts, and a cherry; serve immediately.

Variation:

Pineapple Coconut. Use Pineapple Sauce, page 242, with Banana-Macadamia Frozen Yogurt, page 134.

1 serving (without fudge sauce) contains:

Cal	Carb	Fat	Chol	Calcium
260	25g	17g	49mg	122mg

Praline Parfait

ENJOY THE WONDERFUL TASTE OF PRALINES.

Makes 6 to 8 servings

1	cup packed brown sugar
1/2	cup light corn syrup
1/2	cup half-and-half
1/4	cup butter or margarine
1/2	teaspoon vanilla extract
1/2	cup chopped pecans
1	quart vanilla or coffee ice cream

Whipped cream, if desired

IN A MEDIUM SAUCEPAN, combine brown sugar, corn syrup, half-and-half, and butter or margarine. Stir over low heat until sugar dissolves. Let simmer 5 minutes. Stir in vanilla and pecans. Cool to room temperature. Place 6 to 8 parfait glasses or wine glasses in freezer to chill, at least 30 minutes. Arrange alternate layers of ice cream and sauce in chilled glasses. Cover with foil or plastic wrap. Place in freezer; freeze until firm, 2 to 4 hours. If desired, top each serving with whipped cream.

Variation:

Maple-Walnut. Substitute maple syrup for corn syrup; walnuts for pecans.

1 serving contains:

Cal	Carb	Fat	Chol	Calcium
553	80g	26g	67mg	172mg

Root-Beer Sorbet

UNUSUAL AND SO REFRESHING.

| Makes about 1 quart |

> 2 tablespoons water
> 1 teaspoon unflavored gelatin
> 2 (12-ounce) cans root beer
> 2 tablespoons sugar
> 2 tablespoons light corn syrup

IN A SMALL SAUCEPAN, combine water and gelatin; let stand 1 minute. Heat and stir until gelatin dissolves; remove from heat. In a medium bowl, combine root beer with dissolved gelatin, sugar, and corn syrup. Stir until blended. Pour into ice cream canister. Freeze in ice cream maker according to manufacturer's directions; or follow refrigerator-freezer instructions on page 11.

1 serving contains:

Cal	Carb	Fat	Chol	Calcium
87	22g	0g	0mg	7mg

Almond-Apricot-Brandy Sauce

USE AS A SUNDAE TOPPING OR BETWEEN LAYERS OF ICE CREAM IN A PARFAIT.

Makes about 1¼ cups

- 1 cup apricot jam
- 2 tablespoons orange juice
- ¼ cup chopped almonds, toasted
- 1 tablespoon apricot brandy

IN A SMALL SAUCEPAN, combine apricot jam and orange juice. Stir over low heat until jam dissolves. Stir in almonds and brandy. Serve warm.

1 tablespoon contains:

Cal	Carb	Fat	Chol	Calcium
51	11g	1g	0mg	8mg

Apricot Sauce

GREAT SERVED OVER PINEAPPLE, BANANA, OR OTHER TROPICAL-FRUIT-FLAVORED YOGURTS.

Makes about 1¼ cups

1	tablespoon cornstarch
2	tablespoons sugar
1	cup apricot nectar
¼	cup light corn syrup
1	teaspoon lemon juice

IN SMALL SAUCEPAN, combine cornstarch and sugar. Stir in apricot nectar and corn syrup. Cook and stir over moderate heat until translucent and slightly thickened. Remove from heat. Add lemon juice; cool.

1 tablespoon contains:

Cal	Carb	Fat	Chol	Calcium
25	7g	0g	0mg	1mg

Favorite Fudge Sauce

QUICK TOPPING FOR SUNDAES AND PARFAITS.

Makes about 1 cup

- ½ cup sugar
- ¼ cup unsweetened cocoa powder
- ½ cup light corn syrup
- ¼ cup half-and-half
- 2 tablespoons butter or margarine
- ½ teaspoon vanilla extract

IN A SMALL SAUCEPAN, combine sugar and cocoa. Stir in corn syrup and half-and-half. Stir over medium heat until mixture comes to a boil. Stirring occasionally, simmer 3 minutes. Stir in butter or margarine and vanilla. Serve warm or cold.

1 tablespoon contains:

Cal	Carb	Fat	Chol	Calcium
74	15g	2g	5mg	6mg

Raspberry-Currant Sauce

FOR RASPBERRY-RIPPLE ICE CREAM, SWIRL 1¼ CUPS OF THIS TOPPING INTO ONE QUART OF VANILLA ICE CREAM. QUICK AND EASY TO MAKE, IT'S ALSO A HANDY TOPPING FOR YOGURT SUNDAES AND PARFAITS.

Makes 1 cup

- **2** cups fresh or frozen unsweetened raspberries
- **⅓** cup currant jelly
- **1** tablespoon margarine or butter
- **⅛** teaspoon almond extract

IN BLENDER OR FOOD PROCESSOR fitted with a metal blade, purée berries. Strain; discard seeds. In small saucepan, combine strained berries, currant jelly, and margarine or butter. Stir over low heat until jelly and margarine dissolve. Stir in almond extract; cool to room temperature. Cover and refrigerate until used.

1 tablespoon contains:

Cal	Carb	Fat	Chol	Calcium
31	6g	1g	2mg	4mg

Whipped Yogurt

USE THIS TOPPING WITHIN 24 HOURS AFTER IT'S MADE. OR IT CAN BE FROZEN, THEN THAWED, STIRRED, AND SERVED.

Makes about 1½ cups

2½	tablespoons nonfat dry milk
2	tablespoons nonfat milk
1	egg white
2	tablespoons light corn syrup
½	cup vanilla low-fat yogurt

IN CUSTARD OR MEASURING CUP, combine dry and liquid milk. Stir until dry milk dissolves; set aside in refrigerator. In small mixer bowl, beat egg white with electric mixer on medium-high speed until foamy. Add corn syrup and chilled milk mixture; continue beating until mixture is glossy and soft peaks form. Fold in yogurt. Cover and refrigerate until used or freeze if it will be used more than 24 hours after it is made.

1 tablespoon contains:

Cal	Carb	Fat	Chol	Calcium
14	2g	0g	9mg	17mg

Strawberry Soda

THIS MUST BE SERVED WHILE THE CLUB SODA STILL HAS PLENTY OF BUBBLES.

Makes 2 servings

½ cup cold milk
¼ cup strawberry syrup
4 scoops strawberry ice cream
Cold club soda
Whipped cream
2 maraschino cherries

IN A SMALL BOWL, stir milk into strawberry syrup. Pour evenly into two tall glasses. Add 1 scoop of ice cream to each glass. Pour a small amount of club soda into each glass. Press ice cream into club soda with back of a long-handled spoon. Add second scoop of ice cream to each glass. Fill glasses with soda. Garnish each with whipped cream and a cherry. Serve immediately.

Variations:

Raspberry. Substitute Raspberry-Currant Sauce, page 243, for strawberry syrup. Use strawberry or vanilla ice cream.

Chocolate. Substitute chocolate syrup and chocolate ice cream for strawberry syrup and strawberry ice cream.

1 serving contains:

Cal	Carb	Fat	Chol	Calcium
412	58g	19g	67mg	302mg

Ice Cream After-Dinner Drinks

CHOOSE YOUR FAVORITE FLAVOR.

Makes 2 servings

AMARETTO

- 2 tablespoons Amaretto liqueur
- 1 large scoop vanilla ice cream
- 1 large scoop orange sherbet

Whipped cream

GRASSHOPPER

- 2 tablespoons green crème de menthe
- 2 tablespoons white crème de cocoa
- 2 large scoops vanilla ice cream

Whipped cream

BRANDIED PEACH

- 2 tablespoons brandy
- 2 tablespoons orange-flavored liqueur
- 2 large scoops peach ice cream

Whipped cream

IN BLENDER, combine liqueurs and ice cream or sherbet; blend until smooth. Pour into 2 sherbet glasses or wine glasses. Top with whipped cream.

1 Amaretto serving contains:

Cal	Carb	Fat	Chol	Calcium
201	25g	8g	30mg	72mg

1 Grasshopper serving contains:

Cal	Carb	Fat	Chol	Calcium
311	33g	12g	45mg	107mg

1 Brandied Peach serving contains:

Cal	Carb	Fat	Chol	Calcium
205	21g	9g	37mg	84mg

Bellini Freeze

FROZEN VERSION OF A FAMOUS VENETIAN DRINK.

Makes 8 servings

4	fresh ripe peaches, peeled, sliced
½	cup sugar
2	tablespoons almond liqueur
1	(750-ml) bottle Asti Spumante or other sweet sparkling white wine, chilled

IN BLENDER OR FOOD PROCESSOR fitted with metal blade, purée peaches and sugar. Add almond liqueur; process 2 to 3 seconds to blend. Pour into a 9" x 5" loaf pan. Cover with foil or plastic wrap. Freeze until almost firm, 1 to 3 hours. Cut 3 lengthwise rows and 8 crosswise rows through mixture. Replace cover and freeze until firm, 1 to 3 hours. Place in refrigerator to soften slightly 10 to 15 minutes before serving. To serve, place 3 pieces in each of 8 sherbet glasses or champagne glasses. Pour Asti Spumante or other sweet white wine over frozen mixture. Serve with a spoon.

1 serving contains:

Cal	Carb	Fat	Chol	Calcium
155	22g	0g	0mg	8mg

Frozen Kir Spritzer

TASTES LIKE A WINE COOLER.

Makes 5 or 6 servings

2	cups dry white wine
¼	cup sugar
2	tablespoons lemon juice
½	cup crème de cassis
3	(12-ounce) cans club soda or lemon-lime soda

IN A SMALL SAUCEPAN, combine wine, sugar, and lemon juice. Stir over low heat until sugar dissolves. Cool to room temperature. Stir in cassis. Pour into a 9" x 5" loaf pan or several undivided ice trays. Cover with foil or plastic wrap. Freeze until almost firm, 1 to 3 hours. Break into small pieces. Beat with electric mixer or food processor fitted with a metal blade until fine-grained but not thawed. Return beaten mixture to pan and freeze until almost firm, 1 to 3 hours. To serve, scoop mixture into 5 or 6 tall glasses. Fill glasses with club or lemon-lime soda.

1 serving contains:

Cal	Carb	Fat	Chol	Calcium
203	22g	0g	0mg	20mg

Ice Cream Smoothies

ESPECIALLY GOOD ON A SWELTERINGLY HOT DAY.

Makes 2 or 3 servings

TROPICAL BANANA

- 1 large banana, peeled, diced
- 1 cup milk
- 2 large scoops orange or pineapple sherbet

Dash of ground nutmeg

PIÑA COLADA

- ¼ cup chilled pineapple juice
- 3 tablespoons cream of coconut
- 3 tablespoons rum
- 3 large scoops vanilla ice cream

GREEN SILK

- 1 ripe avocado, peeled, quartered
- ¾ cup chilled pineapple juice
- 4 large scoops orange sherbet

IN BLENDER OR FOOD PROCESSOR fitted with a metal blade, blend ingredients until smooth. Pour into wine or champagne glasses.

1 Tropical Banana serving contains:

Cal	Carb	Fat	Chol	Calcium
234	43g	6g	21mg	187mg

1 Piña Colada serving contains:

Cal	Carb	Fat	Chol	Calcium
360	35g	18g	53mg	159mg

1 Green Silk serving contains:

Cal	Carb	Fat	Chol	Calcium
408	63g	18g	8mg	103mg

Index

C

cakes
  chocolate ice cream roll, 215
  coconut snowballs, 199
  frozen yogurt-raspberry trifle, 228
  ice cream birthday cake, 201
candy
  burnt sugar frozen yogurt, 194
  Butterfinger frozen yogurt, 187
  butterscotch frozen yogurt, 195
  chocolate-mint parfait frozen yogurt, 192
  chocolate-pecan ice cream bonbons, 198
  crunchy toffee bar frozen yogurt, 191
  grasshopper frozen yogurt, 190
  licorice-stick ice cream, 183
  Oreo cookie frozen yogurt, 186
  pastel mint frozen yogurt, 193
  peanut-butter-caramel frozen yogurt, 189
  peanut-butter cups frozen yogurt, 188
  peppermint frozen yogurt, 185
  peppermint-stick ice cream, 184
  Snickers candy ice cream, 181
  toffee-coffee ice cream, 182
cantaloupe
  cantaloupe-orange pops, 209
  cantaloupe sherbet, 154
  cantaloupe-wine sorbet, 155
  ginger-honey-cantaloupe frozen yogurt, 156
  papaya-nut frozen yogurt, 148
cheesecakes
  apricot frozen-yogurt cheesecake, 222
  frozen yogurt Sicilian cheesecake, 44
  lemon cheesecake ice cream, 81
  lime ice cream cheesecake, 223
  mocha ice cream cheesecake, 219
cherries
  bing cherry-cranberry frozen yogurt, 108
  cherries jubilee, 234
  cherry-berry ice cream, 106
  cherry-cranberry sorbet, 107

chocolate. *See also* fudge
  frozen yogurt, 37
  frozen yogurt, delight, 40
  frozen yogurt, semi-sweet fleck, 41
  frozen yogurt, sugar-free, 38
  ice cream, chocolate-chip mint, 33
  ice cream, country, 28
  ice cream, fudge, 30
  ice cream, old-fashioned, 29
  ice cream, rocky road, 31
  ice cream sandwiches, double chocolate, 200
  white chocolate, ice cream, 35
coconut
  Bali Hai banana ice cream, 130
  coconut-cream pineapple frozen yogurt, 136
  coconut custard frozen yogurt, 137
  coconut-macadamia ice cream, 176
  coconut snowballs, 199
  pecan-chocolate crunch ice cream, 173
coffee drinks
  café au lait ice cream, 46
  Irish-coffee ice cream, 48
  latte frozen yogurt, 47
  mocha-bahia frozen yogurt, 45
cranberries
  bing cherry-cranberry frozen yogurt, 108
  cherry-cranberry sorbet, 107
  cranberry-orange sherbet, 76
  cranberry-wine sorbet, 77
  orange-cranberry-nut frozen yogurt, 91
Crenshaw melon. *See* cantaloupe
cups
  orange frozen-yogurt cups, 210
  peach frozen-yogurt cups, 211
custards
  coconut custard frozen yogurt, 137
  peach custard ice cream, 114
  rhubarb custard ice cream, 165

D-E-F

G-H-I

K-L

M-N

O-P-Q

T

V-W-Y